The Competitive Runner's Training Book

The Competitive Runner's Training Book

**Bill Dellinger
and Bill Freeman**

Introduction by Alberto Salazar

A Runner's World Book

*Collier Books
Macmillan Publishing Company
New York*

*Collier Macmillan Publishers
London*

Macmillan Publishing Company
866 Third Avenue, New York, N.Y. 10022
Collier Macmillan Canada, Inc.

Library of Congress Cataloging in Publication Data

Dellinger, Bill.
  The competitive runner's training book.

  "A Runner's world book."
  1. Running—Training.   I. Freeman,
William Hardin, 1943-   . II. Title.
GV1061.5.D45   1984   796.4'26   84-15436
ISBN 0-02-530570-0
ISBN 0-02-028340-7 (pbk.)

Macmillan books are available at special discounts for bulk purchases for sales promotions, premiums, fund-raising, or educational use.

  For details, contact:
Special Sales Director
Macmillan Publishing Company
866 Third Avenue
New York, New York 10022
First Collier Books Edition 1984
10 9 8 7 6
Printed in the United States of America

The Competitive Runner's Training Book is also available in a hardcover edition published by Macmillan Publishing Company.

Cover photo by Jeff Reinking

1980 Olympic Trials photos by David Madison; pg. 37, 89, Warren Morgan; pg. 19, 23, Andy Whipple; pg. 15, courtesy of University of Oregon Archives.

Contents

Acknowledgments

To Bill Bowerman, whose influence on American distance training systems continues to grow, and to our athletes, who are critical to improving any system of training.

Introduction

For many years, runners, coaches and scientists have argued over which method of training is the best. Some insist it's the methodology espoused by Arthur Lydiard; others say it is year-round interval training, while others say the best way to train is by using long, slow distance. It's my belief that there isn't one system or theory that is logically complete and perfect in itself; rather, the best system should be one that takes the best that each has to offer and synthesizes it into a well-rounded, total system.

This is what my long-time coach, Bill Dellinger, has done. He has borrowed from many of the great coaches, such as Lydiard and his predecessor at Oregon, Bill Bowerman, and added many of his own ideas. The result is what has become known as the Oregon System.

Over the years, Dellinger has constantly refined and developed his training methods. Although the late Steve Prefontaine, the first great runner Dellinger coached, followed similar training patterns to what Dellinger-coached runners do now, much has been added. Every year, Dellinger is looking for new ways to improve training, and henceforth, performance. It's the only way for his athletes to keep up with the continual improvements in times. This is illustrated by the fact that Prefontaine's American 5000-meter record at the time of his death was 13:22.4 and yet I have lowered the record to 13:11.9. (The three fastest American 5000-meter times have all been recorded by Dellinger-coached runners: myself, Matt Centrowitz and Bill McChesney.)

Besides incorporating successful training methods, Dellinger has always tried to make running fun and rewarding. If the workouts would always be too hard and unenjoyable, the runners would become stale and irritable. Just this past winter

(1984), Dellinger introduced us to a new facet of winter training: circuit training. It was designed to give us something new and exciting to do, while building up various muscle groups we might have been ignoring. Bill borrowed this concept from the Brazilian coach, Luis de Oliveira, who is the personal coach of Oregon's great 800- and 1500-meter champion, Joaquim Cruz.

Dellinger's Oregon System is in a continual state of change. Bill is the only constant. He's constantly improving and tinkering with the Oregon System as well as molding it to allow for the different characteristics of his runners. For instance, while I was competing at Oregon with Rudy Chapa, a NCAA 5000-meter champion, Dellinger allowed us to do about half of our training together. The remaining portion was individually tailored to each of our strengths. In my case, endurance and in Rudy's, his speed.

I believe that this book will enable any runner to have the best training methods in the world presented in a simple, yet flexible format that can be adjusted to the individual. Bill has been a great coach for me; I'm certain his knowledge and experience can be beneficial for recreational runners as well.

Alberto Salazar
Eugene, Oregon
July 1984

1. The Principles of Good Training

Successful running requires a good training program. No single program is the perfect way to train: You can use many different routes to the same goal. However, every successful training program follows certain basic principles and shares common characteristics with the other successful training programs. At the University of Oregon, first we set goals we want to reach, then we develop a program based on our "Five Training Principles."

GOAL-ORIENTED RUNNING

The first necessity for a good training program is to have a clear goal. It is hard to get somewhere if you have no idea where you are going. Goals are like road maps: Once you know where you want to go, you can consider the routes that will get you there, and choose the best one.

Progressing from your present physical condition to a higher level is like driving from one city to another. Usually you can choose several routes to get there. You might choose one route because it looks more interesting. You might choose another for special reasons: If you have an aging car or heavy truck, you might take a longer route that avoids the hills. Planning your training is very similar.

Your goal may be to reach a certain level of performance at a specific distance, such as the mile or a 10-kilometer road race. On the other hand, your goal may be to qualify for an important race, such as the Boston Marathon or the NCAA 10,000 meters. Remember, the best way to get there is to have a clear goal.

Your goal should be challenging, but realistic. If you have run a 5:00 mile, a goal of 4:58 is hardly a challenge. On the other hand, a goal of 4:00 for the next year is unrealistic. Base your goal on your competitive record and training and racing experience. A new runner will make bigger improvements than an experienced one because the early gains come much more easily.

You may want to have more than one goal. When you run on a team, you may have a goal for the competitive season and another for the whole year. Older runners may have a goal for the season and another goal for the next year or several years. This is a wise course to follow, but remember that long-term goals need to be reconsidered each year, based on last year's performance.

THE FIVE TRAINING PRINCIPLES

When you plan a training program, keep the Five Training Principles in mind. They are: 1) moderation, 2) progression, 3) adaptability, 4) variation, and 5) the callousing effect. Let's look more closely at what each means to the overall training program.

1. Moderation. Moderation is the most critical part of any new runner's training program. You'll probably want to see how hard you can train, or how many miles you can run in a week. People are naturally competitive and looking for the best training system. This drive often leads slower runners to imitate faster runners' training methods, one of the most common mistakes runners make.

Two big problems of the new runner (and the experienced runner) are injury and burnout. Their most common cause is overtraining. "It is better to undertrain than to overtrain," runners are frequently told at the University of Oregon. Many runners and coaches find this idea hard to believe, but the historical evidence is overwhelming. For example, in the 1930s Glenn Cunningham ran a 4:04 mile indoors while running 15 to 20 miles a week — typical training mileage for American runners of that era.

To make sure you aren't running too hard, try the "talk test." You should be able to carry on a conversation while running; if you cannot, you are running too fast. For most workouts, this is true even for elite runners. Of course, elite runners will be able to carry on a conversation while running at a much faster pace. If you watch a marathon or long track race on television, you may see racers who appear to be talking, which frequently is what they're doing. You should run within your capacity, not push yourself to the edge.

Elite runners at the University of Oregon do some very hard workouts. These workouts are done only occasionally (several weeks apart) in their training. In fact, training too hard can be worse than no training at all. The stress of hard running makes you more likely to become sick or injured. Frequent colds or minor, nagging injuries are common signs of overtraining, as are the feelings of always being a little tired, muscle cramps or blood in the urine. Consequently, it pays to monitor your body closely.

After most workouts you should feel refreshed, not tired. A hard workout will leave you feeling pleasantly fatigued. Moderation should always be your first training principle.

2. Progression. Some runners overlook the very important principle of progression — gradual change. You should improve your physical condition gradually and start with modest goals. For example, track runners may begin interval work at their slowest pace in August or September, increasing the pace regularly throughout the training year, until they reach a peak in June or July.

Many runners have a problem controlling their training progression and peak too soon. If you are running your most important race in May or June, you don't want to run your fastest times in March or April, as many racers do. We try to control a runner's progress by using Date Pace and Goal Pace when doing interval training.

Goal Pace is the speed you want to run at the end of your

season. If your goal is a 5:00 mile, your Goal Pace for 440 yards is 75 seconds. At that pace, you should run your mile in five minutes.

Date Pace is how fast you can run the distance now. If you can run a 5:40 mile, then your Date Pace is 85 seconds for 440 yards.

Establish your Date Pace with a moderate-effort time trial early in the year. Then you may increase your pace about every three weeks, doing the most intervals at Date Pace. Finish the three-week training period with a medium-effort time trial at the Date Pace. If you can complete the distance at that speed, your Date Pace should increase for the next 21-day training cycle. If you cannot run at the Date Pace speed, the pace should remain the same.

At the University of Oregon we also look at the runner's progression in time trials and races during the year. We will mark the first time trial and the goal for the year on a sheet of graph paper (Figure 2). We then mark in each race and time trial, which show us how the runners are progressing toward their goals.

3. Adaptability. You must learn to adapt to changing situations if you hope to run well. Adaptability applies primarily to the coach. If you are self-coached, you should use common sense to adapt to the weather, your state of health, and any other circumstances that might affect your training. You won't have the same training conditions as other runners. Some people have ideal places to train, but others have poor locations or climates. You must know what is available and adapt your training program to take advantage of it.

Some distance runners live in cool climates ideal for running; however, not all races will be in cool climates, so you may be able to gain an advantage from your training if you live and race in a warm climate. If you have no hills to train on, you need to find other types of training to simulate hill running, just as a runner in very hilly areas has to find a substitute for running on flat terrain. Adaptability will also apply to your racing, as you work to take advantage of your assets. You cannot expect ideal training or racing conditions. The runner who

Bill Dellinger ran for the University of Oregon during his competitive years in the mid-1950s.

expects the ideal will be more easily distracted when he encounters poor terrain or bad weather in a race, and his performance will suffer.

After graduating from college in the late 1950s, I was assigned to a radar base on an isolated part of the Washington coastline. I had no track or measured roads to train on, only the beach. I adapted by counting strides and estimating the distance of one stride. Each time my right foot touched the sand, it counted as one stride. I used my fingers to represent paired strides. Each finger represented 10 strides. I estimated how many strides I needed for the different training intervals (typical track distances like 440 yards), then ran timed intervals on the beach, counting steps as I ran.

After a year of this unconventional training, I set a number of personal records on the track, several which were American records. By adapting my training to my environment, rather than seeking ideal training conditions, I was able to run to my potential as well as fulfill my military duties.

A coach needs to remember the importance of confidence to a runner's potential for success. When a runner has successful workouts, he gains confidence. If the runner cannot handle the workout, he loses confidence. The fault will be with the coach, not the athlete. A coach needs to be able to perceive when a workout is too hard or unreasonable for the conditions so he can modify it to the runner's abilities.

In my later training years, I only saw my coach, Bill Bowerman, about once a month. So each week I wrote down a workout that I felt was consistent with Bowerman's training principles and my own needs. I adapted his plan to the training conditions and my fitness level. If I planned to run five-mile-repeats in 4:30, but it was raining hard, I knew the workout was unreasonable for the conditions. I would do a different workout instead.

Ten days before Alberto Salazar's best 10-kilometer race, I scheduled a workout of six-times-one-mile in 4:20 as a confidence builder. By the fifth mile, Salazar was looking tired, so after his recovery interval, I changed the last mile interval to 5×330 in 48 seconds; although Salazar needed to do a full workout for his confidence, he couldn't handle the one planned, so it was changed. The change didn't make the workout easier or shorter, simply more realistic.

Too many runners and coaches look at a workout as a challenge that must be met regardless of conditions, as if it is chiseled in stone. In truth, any workout is merely a means to running a successful race. A workout that defeats the runner fails in its purpose. There are no magic workouts, no "If you can do this workout, you will run that time" training sessions. The human body does not function exactly like a machine. You must be able to adapt the training program to your needs and conditions on a daily basis, rather than expecting your program to stand apart as an idealized goal. A good workout should be a challenge, but an attainable one.

4. Variation. Variety is the spice of training as much as of life itself. You want to avoid getting into a training rut. If every Monday means 12 × 440 on the track, it won't be long before you lose interest in training. You should seek a variety of places to train — roads, parks, woods, hiking trails, and so on.

You need to vary your training program to meet your needs. At times you may need to concentrate on speed, or perhaps long intervals for endurance. Having variety in training locales, workout sessions and training intensity will keep you mentally fresher, just as your body will be strengthened.

Using Date Pace and Goal Pace in interval training will help meet this need for variety. Although your Date Pace will change regularly as you improve during the year, your Goal Pace will remain the same until the two paces merge at the appointed time. Most training sessions will use Date Pace, but some will use Goal Pace. This method allows your body to become familiar with the tempo of Goal Pace. Your sense of pace judgment will also improve from training at a variety of speeds. You must learn to recognize and control pace changes.

Variation is also achieved with the hard/easy training pattern: a period of intense or "hard" training followed by a period of recovery or "easy" training. You will improve only for a short time and then get worse if you don't take a break from hard training. The recovery or rest periods are as important as the hard training periods, because the body is given a chance to adjust to the harder training.

5. Callousing Effect. The fifth training principle is the Callousing Effect. Basically, this means doing things in your training that will make you mentally and physically tougher. Your body needs to develop resistance to the stress of high-level competition, which is not achieved in most training sessions. Doing a workout that pushes you well beyond what you're used to is one method of getting "calloused."

You may encounter a number of different racing tactics that involve changes of speed or greater effort at unexpected places in the race. With this in mind, you need to practice racing methods you might use or that might be used against you. A racing tactic becomes a useful weapon merely because of the element of surprise, or because competitors can't cope with the pace.

The Callousing Effect should begin with the weather, because you can never pick the weather for an outdoor race. You must be prepared to race in whatever weather you encounter.

The running surface may also be a factor. You may encounter very difficult terrain in cross-country races, ranging from soggy or sandy ground to steep hills, which may not be to your liking. Though more and more running tracks are all-weather, many cinder and dirt tracks are used. The condition of these tracks varies considerably, depending upon how well they're maintained and the weather.

The time of day a race is held can be a factor also. The time of day you feel strongest may not coincide with the time of your race. Most track races are held in the afternoon, yet in large meets you might compete at any time from 8:00 in the morning to 10:00 or later at night. Road races and marathons are usually held in the morning, starting as early at 6:00 or as late as noon. In planning your major race, find out the time it will be held and then train at that time of day, if possible. If a race is at dawn, your body must accustom itself to running hard at that time.

At major track meets, you may have to run a series of qualifying races before the finals. For example, in the 1984 U.S. Olympic Trials and in the Olympic Games, men in the 5000 meters ran three races in four days. Although the first race

Rudy Chapa speeds around Hayward Field's Stevenson Track on record pace during a 5000-meter race in 1979. The stadium on the University of Oregon campus seats 14,200.

may not require your best performance, none of the races will be easy; the cumulative effect of ever-faster races with little rest will take its toll. You must begin training months in advance to simulate racing conditions of this sort, rather than hope that by doing enough mileage you will be able to withstand the stress.

The Callousing Effect might be likened to going the "extra mile" in training. You're trying to throw in that little bit of extra intensity that will see you through the hard races. It is perhaps the final training aspect to help you achieve your potential. Because the intense workout causes more stress, it should be done only once every several weeks.

Now that we have discussed the need for goals in running and the Five Training Principles, the types of training used by runners follow.

2. The Types of Training

OVERDISTANCE RUNNING: BUILDING A BASE

The part of training often called the "base" — the training foundation — is critical to successful racing. If you want to run very fast or very often, a strong foundation of training is necessary. Think of this base in terms of miles per week covered over an extended period of time, at least several months. The purpose of the base is to enhance your strength, endurance, and cardio-respiratory system.

This does not mean that a person cannot race successfully on low mileage. As we mentioned earlier, men have run close to four minutes for a mile on very low mileage. Bill Bowerman's stable of sub-4:00 milers at Oregon generally averaged 60 miles per week. The difference of the higher mileage or higher intensity training shows in today's more intensive racing schedules.

Even in the 1950s and 1960s, there were few quality races for the American runner. A sub-4:00 miler might run only one or two high-caliber races a year, with most races more or less time trials by comparison. Today, a typical college track racing season for a national-level competitor is three months, six months if the runner also races indoors. Few of these races are low-key, "easy" meets. A world-class miler might run one dozen to two dozen mile races in 3:55 or faster during a single season from January until September. No athlete can run such a racing schedule purely on low mileage and natural talent.

The higher intensity of training in the 1980s has permitted the athlete to run fast and often. Notice the word "intensity," rather than mileage. Mileage is not the sole (or even the best) measure of a high-level training program. Every runner needs to remember that the quality of training is as important as the quantity.

The 1970s may have been the high-water mark for high-mileage training by distance runners. Recently, training has tended to emphasize higher quality and fewer miles, but many runners still do high mileage. There is no single popular training plan among world-class runners; many plans are followed, and they are evolving continually. However, more athletes are using the hard/easy system in various forms.

You can balance mileage and intensity in your training, as Figure 1 shows. Instead of a jog or slow run of 20 or more miles, you might do a faster run of 8 to 15 miles, or a type of fartlek workout that more carefully controls the overall quality of the workout. As you increase the intensity of your training sessions, you should decrease your weekly mileage to avoid more stress.

There are no hard rules for how much mileage or intensity you need in your training. The best rule to follow is: Listen to your body. Do not try to force your body past its limits. Hard training requires working the body and testing it, but it should be pushed to the limit only rarely. Allow enough recovery to permit your body to adapt and strengthen itself between those high-intensity efforts. Research shows that you will need from 24 to 72 hours to recover from a hard workout, depending upon how hard it is and your physical condition at the time.

Though more runners now mix their types of training throughout the year, many runners emphasize the base period to get a number of weeks or months of training at a certain mileage level. In the Northern Hemisphere these are most often the fall and winter months. If cross-country is a serious racing season like track, then this base period might run from late November to February or March.

Though many collegiate runners compete in cross-country in

the fall, indoor track in the winter and track in the spring and summer, it is not the wisest plan for your long-term development as a runner. The body needs an off-season and base training period. Though the trend at the highest levels is toward more and more races, it is not conducive to better times. Indeed, you will run faster with more training time and fewer races.

A common base training pattern among college runners is to use the summer months to prepare for cross-country season, and December until March for the outdoor track season. The mileage and intensity levels of the base periods will depend upon your age, experience, talent and planning. It should never be decided merely by going out and seeing "how much I can take."

Though you will hear many types of training described, the choices are simpler than most people realize. There are only two types of training: continuous running and interrupted running. All types of training are variations of one of those two types. Continuous running breaks down to types of training called long runs, steady runs, mileage, Lydiard fartlek, tempo runs, LSD (long, slow distance), and many others. Interrupted or non-continuous running includes such well-known workouts as interval training and fartlek. Let's look at each of the major types of training in more detail.

INTERVAL TRAINING

Interval training, as we know it, was developed largely by Dr. Woldemar Gerschler of Germany in the 1930s, along with cardiologist Dr. Herbert Reindell. Intervals became very popular in the United States in the 1950s and 1960s, in two different versions.

The first version, which we'll call "pure" interval training, always calls for relatively fast, short intervals. It is "quality" running designed to build endurance and strength through many repeated short runs. The second version, from which we get "Date Pace," was developed by Franz Stampfl in England in the early 1950s. It is based on the idea of starting at a certain pace early in the year, then gradually running the intervals faster as the year progresses, until the intervals are being run as fast as your goal for the year.

Interval training is defined as running short distances a number of times during a workout. Interval training has five variations that determine the difficulty of the workout:

1. length of the interval (time or distance run);
2. intensity of the effort (speed or effort of the run);
3. number of intervals;
4. length of the recovery (time of rest intervals); and
5. the type of recovery (jogging, walking, or complete rest).

Dellinger holds the ubiquitous stopwatch so familiar to Alberto Salazar and other Oregon team members during an interval workout.

Pure interval training is always short intervals, usually a distance that takes from 15 seconds to one minute to run, with a rest interval of 45 to 90 seconds. Gerschler recommended intervals of about 200, 150 or 100 meters. Each interval should raise the heart rate to near-maximum (about 180), and the recovery phase allows the pulse rate to drop to about 120 to 125 beats per minute. In essence, the intervals are repeated until the heart rate does not drop into the low range within 90 seconds. The real work or adaptation by the body takes place during the recovery periods, not during the runs.

Interval training includes both speed (anaerobic) training and endurance (aerobic) training. Anaerobic training is running done at such a fast pace that the body cannot take in the oxygen it needs until after the run is completed. Aerobic running occurs when you can take in as much oxygen as you need during the run. The determining factor is your running pace: When you cannot continue running without slowing down, you have switched from aerobic to anaerobic training. The distinction between speed and endurance training is not just the speed or length of the interval; the number of repetitions is a factor. If you can do an interval a dozen times, your aerobic condition, not your speed is affected. At the same time, as your aerobic system improves, so does your speed, because the better your endurance, the longer you can run at a pace close to your top speed.

Runners prefer looking at only two components of energy needed for a race: anaerobic and aerobic energy. The shorter and faster a run, the less it involves taking in and using oxygen. Though it is a very rough estimate, the proportions needed for different races are as follows:

Distance	Anaerobic	Aerobic
800	67%	33%
1500	45%	55%
5 km	20%	80%
10 km	10%	90%
Marathon	2%	98%

The top international distance runners are using more fast or anaerobic training than this table suggests.

At Oregon we use two terms for variations of intervals — interval training and repetition training. For us, the difference lies in the emphasis. In interval training, as we define it, we are controlling the rest period. Though we may run the intervals increasingly faster, as with "cut-downs," the rest duration will remain the same. With repetition runs, the object is to match the time: The length of the recovery is not important. Though it is not always the case, we do repetition runs most often when we are doing speedwork, as when I had Matt Centrowitz run 4 × 440 in 52 seconds as speedwork for the 5000-meter run. In such a workout, it doesn't matter how long the rest is: The important thing is hitting the 52-second target.

Most coaches will distinguish between the terms interval and repetition running by the length of the interval, but by our definition many shorter intervals can be called repetition training, and one-mile repeats can be interval training. We usually run mile repeats with either a 440-yard jog or a three-minute rest, making it interval training by our definition.

Interval training can have a number of different emphases. It can be used to develop pace judgment, as in the use of Goal Pace, Date Pace and cut-down intervals; to improve the aerobic capacity or the anaerobic component; to increase the intensity of training or simulate parts of a race. Its greatest value, perhaps, is that you can be very specific in designing your training load. Thus, you can be very precise about how hard you train in a given session. This is not so true of other types of training. We will discuss intervals a bit more when we talk about pace training.

FARTLEK

Fartlek is a Swedish term that means "speed play." It is a free-form version of interval training designed to be used away from the track, ideally on trails or across open terrain. It was developed by Gosta Holmer and was the central feature of much of Scandinavian running success earlier in this century. It only reached the United States in the late 1940s, after it was described accurately and in detail by *Track and Field News* in a series of articles.

It has always been a confusing concept to American runners. How do you perform a fartlek workout session? Many runners believe any long jog away from the track or road is a fartlek run, but it's not. At Oregon we have added to the confusion by using two different forms of fartlek, which we call 1) varied fartlek, or true fartlek, and 2) Lydiard fartlek, which is not really fartlek.

When we refer to Lydiard fartlek, we're giving credit to Arthur Lydiard of New Zealand for his contributions to training, particularly the idea of longer runs at a steady pace. This steady pace is closer to a "tempo" run; though it is not a fast pace, neither is it a jog, nor a short, easy run. Lydiard fartlek should require some effort to maintain the pace, though it is not supposed to be a hard effort. This type of run is marked in the workout schedules as "steady run (Lydiard fartlek)." Though it is not really fartlek, we are accustomed to calling it by that name. It is an Oregon tradition.

True fartlek is done at a varied pace, most often away from the track. The benefits of fartlek are: 1) We have found that fewer athletes are injured using fartlek training than using other training methods, and 2) it is less boring than other methods. You avoid the monotony of long interval sessions on the track, at the same time avoiding the equally monotonous running of mile after mile on the roads.

Fartlek consists of runs of 20 minutes to an hour, preferably on open terrain having a soft surface, with a sprinkling of faster-paced efforts (or intervals, if your prefer) during the run. Thus, the pace of the run is never the same. The terrain gives variety to the workout.

The main rule of the fartlek workout, however, is simple: Know what you want to do before you start. You may want to run a set number of fast bursts for a certain time or distance during the session. When you start without a plan, you often get little accomplished other than what we call "American fartlek": a medium-length run at a slow pace with a maximum of two short bursts as a gesture of good intentions.

A fartlek run begins with easy-paced running until you feel you've warmed up enough for faster efforts. For the rest of the workout, you have any number of options. You can run the faster bursts by time or distance, like 30 seconds or 200 meters of hard running. The length or duration of the faster pace depends upon your needs. If you need more endurance, you might run longer portions of fast running; if you need speed, run shorter and faster sections. You might work harder on the flat areas, the uphills, the downhills, or any mix of those possibilities.

Though fartlek is basically an unstructured or free-form interval training, many top-level runners are using it in more structured forms, giving it names such as controlled fartlek, extended fartlek, Polish fartlek, and so on. These are much stricter forms of fartlek. For example, you might specify that when you begin the hard, middle part of the session you will run hard for 30 seconds, followed by 30 seconds of easy recovery running, and repeat the effort 12 times. This allows the runner or coach to be more precise about the quality of the session, while avoiding the temptation to let the workout turn into an easy jog.

Fartlek is valuable because of its flexibility. It gives you as many options as you can imagine. You should finish a hard fartlek session tired, but invigorated. You can run easier fartlek sessions as part of a single day's training. Many of our workout sessions on hard-effort days will include 20 minutes of light fartlek, which becomes a pleasant break during a session of intervals on the track. Fartlek, mixed with track intervals, is the heart of the University of Oregon's training system.

TEMPO RUNNING

Tempo running is faster-paced running over a distance, whether run on track, trail or road. It is running at a steady but quick pace over a longer distance, most often 2 to 10 miles (3 to 16 km). Tempo running is being used more by elite runners to fill the gap between aerobic and anaerobic training. It allows the runner to train over longer distances at efforts that simulate the intensity of the race. Tempo running can build both strength and confidence as a runner learns that what was once considered a moderate race pace for a long run may now only be a hard training session.

The diagram below shows the progression in quality or intensity of long runs, from an easy jog up to an intense distance run. Each type of run plays a part in training. We speak of the increase in the intensity of training, but there are limits to any athlete's capacity to benefit from harder training.

Progression in Quality of Long Run

Jogging and LSD ⟶ Steady run ⟶ Tempo run

If an athlete uses more intense training, such as tempo runs, he needs to keep a close watch on his body's reactions to the training. If the symptoms of injury, illness, or constant fatigue appear, the training is too severe. Regardless of the training plan used, there are practical limits to the work you can do and to the rate of improvement you can make in your training and racing abilities in a short time.

PACE TRAINING

Interval training is often used largely as a way of getting a certain amount of work done as well as developing a sense of pace in the runner. At Oregon we work most often with Date Pace and Goal Pace. As mentioned earlier, they mean what they say: Goal Pace is the pace you will be running when you reach your goal, and Date Pace is the pace you can run right now.

At Oregon we usually express these paces as a time for 440 yards or 400 meters. Distances are given in yards and miles because many tracks, including the one at Oregon, are still quarter-mile (440-yard) tracks, though all newer and international tracks are 400 meters; the metric distance is about 2.5 yards less than 440 yards. Running a mile on a 400-meter track requires nearly 10 more meters after four laps (1609 + meters total).

If you are trying to run a 5:00 mile, your Goal Pace is 75 seconds on a 440-yard track. Running 75 seconds per lap for four laps will give you a five-minute mile. For longer distances you may want to express your pace over kilometers or miles. In most American marathons, for example, the "split" times are given at intervals of one or five miles. Most foreign races give splits at intervals of one or five kilometers. For this reason, we have provided some pace charts in the appendices.

At Oregon we usually base the Date Pace at the start of the year on a Trial Effort, which is not run at top speed. We do not want a runner to start the year training very close to Goal Pace. This prevents recovery from the previous season and makes it harder to build gradually toward the next season.

DRILLS

Drills are very useful for simulating the conditions of a hard race or teaching a skill needed in successful racing. We use drills to teach steeplechasers to hurdle, to teach competitors in field events their skills, and to teach runners how to run different parts of their races. Most of the drills you will see in the following workout patterns are designed to simulate the race by having the runner cover portions of the racing distance at goal pace. Other parts of the run are done at a slower pace, so the runner can finish the full racing distance. During the year the fast parts gradually become longer and the easy parts shorter, until the runner is ready to run the race most or all of the way at the Goal Pace.

Figure 1: *Training Mileage and Intensity for the Same Performance Level*

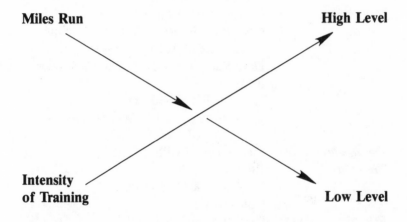

TRAINING PATTERNS

Some people wonder about the training patterns we use at Oregon, the three-week or 21-day pattern for the noncompetitive season, the two-week or 14-day pattern used during the major part of the racing season, and the 10-day pattern used to prepare for the most important races. These patterns were developed at Oregon by Bill Bowerman (based on Gosta Holmer's 10-day pattern) and have continued to be refined by myself. They are the result of almost 40 years of training and racing experience by Oregon runners. Oregon runners use the training schedules to insure variety and progression toward goals in the program.

Though specific workouts are given later, you'll learn their general format here. These training samples or patterns are not law; you will see numerous variations or deviations from these patterns. The pattern is a model, but the workout is the model adapted to the needs of a specific athlete training for a specific race.

Four patterns are given here: 1) the 21-day non-competitive pattern, 2) the 14-day competitive season pattern, 3) the 14-day cross-country season pattern, and 4) the 10-day major competition pattern.

The 21-Day Pattern

Sunday	*(1)*	Steady run (Lydiard fartlek): 6-15 miles [10-25 km.]
Monday	*(2)*	fartlek (Varied fartlek)
Tuesday	*(3)*	Goal Pace Intervals (Usually totaling one mile or 1600 meters) Date Pace Intervals (Usually 2-3 miles or 3-5 km.) Easy fartlek (20-30 min.) Cut-downs (Usually 800-1600 meters or one mile)
Wednesday	*(4)*	Steady run (Lydiard fartlek)
Thursday	*(5)*	Rhythm Easy fartlek (20-30 min.) Cut-downs
Friday	*(6)*	Easy fartlek
Saturday	*(7)*	Overdistance Trial Steady run (Lydiard fartlek) Cut-downs
Sunday	*(8)*	Steady run (Lydiard fartlek): 6-15 miles [10-25 km.]
Monday	*(9)*	fartlek (Varied fartlek)
Tuesday	*(10)*	Hard intervals Easy fartlek (20-30 min.) Cut-downs
Wednesday	*(11)*	Steady run (Lydiard fartlek)
Thursday	*(12)*	Quick running Easy fartlek (20-30 min.) Cut-downs

Friday	*(13)*	Easy fartlek (20-30 min.)
Saturday	*(14)*	Underdistance Trial (shorter than your preferred event)
		Date Pace Intervals
		Easy fartlek (20-30 min.)
		Cut-downs
Sunday	*(15)*	Steady run (Lydiard fartlek): 6-15 miles [10-25 km.]
Monday	*(16)*	fartlek (Varied fartlek)
Tuesday	*(17)*	Goal Pace Intervals
		Steady run (Lydiard fartlek)
		Cut-downs
Wednesday	*(18)*	Steady run (Lydiard fartlek)
Thursday	*(19)*	Quick running
		Easy fartlek (20-30 min.)
		Cut-downs or Simulated Race Drill
Friday	*(20)*	Easy fartlek (20-30 min.)
Saturday	*(21)*	Date Pace Trial
		Steady run (Lydiard fartlek)
		Cut-downs

The 14-Day Pattern

Sunday	*(1)*	Steady run (Lydiard fartlek): 6-15 miles [10-25 km.]
Monday	*(2)*	Easy fartlek (Varied fartlek) (20-30 min.)
Tuesday	*(3)*	Goal Pace Intervals
		Date Pace Intervals
		Easy fartlek (20-30 min.)
Wednesday	*(4)*	Easy steady run (Lydiard fartlek) (20-30 min.)
Thursday	*(5)*	Rhythm or quick running
		fartlek
		Cut-downs
Friday	*(6)*	Easy fartlek (Varied fartlek)
Saturday	*(7)*	Overdistance run
		Underdistance run
		Date Pace Intervals
		fartlek (Varied fartlek)

Sunday	*(8)*	Steady run (Lydiard fartlek): 6-15 miles [10-25 km.]
Monday	*(9)*	Easy fartlek (Varied fartlek) (20-30 min.)
Tuesday	*(10)*	Goal Pace intervals Steady run (Lydiard fartlek) Easy running (20-30 min.)
Wednesday	*(11)*	Easy steady run (Lydiard fartlek) (20-30 min.)
Thursday	*(12)*	Quick running Easy fartlek (Varied fartlek) (20-30 min.) Cut-downs or Simulated Race Drill
Friday	*(13)*	Easy fartlek (Varied fartlek) (20-30 min.)
Saturday	*(14)*	Date Pace Trial Steady run (Lydiard fartlek) Cut-downs

---

The 14-Day Cross-Country Pattern

Sunday	*(1)*	Steady run (Lydiard fartlek): 6-15 miles [10-25 km.]
Monday	*(2)*	Easy fartlek (Varied fartlek) (20-30 min.)
Tuesday	*(3)*	Cut-down intervals Date Pace Intervals Easy fartlek (Varied fartlek) (20-30 min.) Cut-downs
Wednesday	*(4)*	Easy steady run (Lydiard fartlek) (20-30 min.)
Thursday	*(5)*	Intervals on hills Easy fartlek (Varied fartlek) (20-30 min.)
Friday	*(6)*	Easy fartlek (Varied fartlek) (20-30 min.)
Saturday	*(7)*	Overdistance interval Race Simulation Drill fartlek (Varied fartlek)

Sunday	(8)	Steady run (Lydiard fartlek): 6-15 miles [10-25 km.]
Monday	(9)	Easy fartlek over hills (Varied fartlek) (20-30 min.)
Tuesday	(10)	Date Pace intervals Steady run (Lydiard fartlek) Cut-downs
Wednesday	(11)	Easy steady run (Lydiard fartlek) (20-30 min.)
Thursday	(12)	Quick intervals Easy fartlek (Varied fartlek) (20-30 min.) Cut-downs
Friday	(13)	Easy fartlek (Varied fartlek) (20-30 min.)
Saturday	(14)	RACE or Trial

The 10-Day Major Race Pattern

Thursday	(1)	Cut-down intervals Easy run (20-30 min.)
Friday	(2)	Easy run (20-30 min.)
Saturday	(3)	Underdistance trial or Race Simulation Drill Easy steady run (Lydiard fartlek) (20-30 min.) Cut-downs
Sunday	(4)	Easy run (20-30 min.)
Monday	(5)	Easy steady run (Lydiard fartlek) (20-30 min.) Easy quick-interval drills
Tuesday	(6)	Goal Pace intervals Easy run (20-30 min.)
Wednesday	(7)	Easy run (20-30 min.)
Thursday	(8)	Easy run (if no trial-heat races) (20-30 min.)
Friday	(9)	Easy run (20-30 min.)
Saturday	(10)	RACE

3. Building a Training Plan

Now that we have discussed the basic principles of training and the types of training you can use in your program, we need to look at how you can develop your own personal training plan. If you only want to run for exercise, you don't need a highly detailed training plan, though you will still find the training principles presented here valuable. But if you plan to race at any level, whether on a school or club team, as a masters runner, or simply for your own enjoyment, you will be more successful (and enjoy your running more) if you develop a basic training plan and follow it. Building a training plan has several important facets.

GOAL-ORIENTED RUNNING

Your running will be more meaningful if you set goals. Your goal should be a challenge, but a realistic one. There is no value to setting an impossible goal or one that could take many years to reach.

Think of goals as you would a stairway. The stairway reaches from the ground floor to the top floor. When you walk up the stairway, you do not complain that you cannot reach the top floor with only one step, because you know that the distance is too great. It takes a number of steps; the higher you want to go, the more steps you must climb to get there.

Running is a process of gradual improvement. Intermediate goals will help you to get to your long-term goal. You might have one goal for this season, a higher goal for the year, and an even higher one for two years from now.

The important thing is to have a clear goal or set of goals that is realistic, and then to plan carefully how you will achieve those goals. Although it is not true that we can do absolutely anything if our determination is strong enough, most of us are capable of doing far more than we believe we can do.

By setting intermediate goals, you can reach your potential. When you see or read about a world-class runner, remember that often he has trained and raced for up to 10 years to reach that level of skill. He went through the same process of setting intermediate goals, then gradually revising and reaching higher goals.

What should your goal be? To determine your starting goals, ask yourself these questions: How old am I? How long have I been training and racing? What times have I run so far? If you have not run races or trained regularly, the training program in Chapter 7 will help you to get started.

If you have not run before, your first goal should not be race-oriented. Instead, try to train on a regular schedule, such as building up to running five days every week for a month. Your goal might be to run for a certain length of time: 20 minutes, 30 minutes, an hour. The goal should be continuous running, not running a particular distance. For a beginner, a 20- or 30-minute run can be as worthy and satisfying as a good 10,000-meter race for an elite runner. Remember that your goal is for you, based upon your present ability and experience.

If you run for a school team, talk to your coach about your goals and what you hope to do. If he has coached you before, he can make valuable suggestions about which goals are reasonable. Don't feel that if a coach suggests a goal below your expectations, the coach has no confidence in you. Your coach knows that for goals to help in training, they must be attainable. If you're halfway through the year and not progressing as quickly as you hoped, knowing this can be discouraging and hurt your progress even more.

Nothing succeeds like success, so give yourself a chance for the small successes. As long as you don't make them too easy, they will lead to bigger successes down the road.

If you are a beginning runner, it may be best to set only short-term goals, say for this term, season or semester. It is harder to know how far or how quickly you can progress when you are new to an activity. If you are a more experienced runner, you should plan your goals ahead for a full year. The most experienced runners will have goals or targets set from two to four years ahead. Long-term goals along with short-term goals help you to see more clearly where you want to go, so you can keep track of your progress.

Planning Your Progression Toward the Goal

Now that you have set a goal, how are you going to get there? Goals are made so that 1) you can plan your program to get your goal, 2) you can tell how close you are to the goal and 3) you will know when you have reached the goal so you can set a higher one.

First, you need to know your present condition. At Oregon, we have our athletes run a time trial, usually early in December after the fall cross-country season. This trial was described earlier. It is used to set a starting point for your progression. It is never an "all-out" run; instead, we suggest a starting pace that will hold the runners back a bit, allowing them to finish as quickly as they wish over the last lap or two of the trial.

When you have a time for the starting point and a goal for the end of the year, you can then plot your progression on a sheet of graph paper. Put the weeks of the training year across the bottom and the times of the race up the side. Plot the starting (Date) and finishing (Goal) points on the graph and connect them with a dotted line. This gives you an idealized picture of how you hope to progress toward your goal. It will show how fast you should be running three months from now, as well as when you reach your goal. (See Fig. 2, pg. 41)

Each time you run a race at the distance of the goal on your map, put the time down and plot where it falls on the graph. Then draw a solid line from the last race or time trial to the new mark. You will notice your progress doesn't follow a

Matt Centrowitz was a protege of Dellinger's in the late 1970s at the University of Oregon. The two-time Olympian set numerous middle-distance records on the Oregon training system.

straight line. Instead, it will wander above and below the dotted line. As long as you are reasonably close to the line and improving, you are doing well.

Some runners will use J. Gerry Purdy's scoring tables to follow their progress. (James B. Gardner and J. Gerry Purdy. *Computerized Running Training Program.* Los Altos, CA: Tafnews Press, 1970.) His computerized scoring tables are based on the fatigue curve; this method gives him a reasonably close estimate of how fast a runner might run one distance, based on his performance at another distance. A useful feature of the tables is that you can plot your progress based on the point tables, allowing you to record every race and trial on a single sheet of graph paper, regardless of the length of the race.

When tracking your progress with Purdy's tables, remember they are based more on science than reality. They tell which times are at an equal level of skill assuming you are equally good at all of the distances, which is not likely to be true. Still, they are very handy for equating a performance at one distance to a performance at another distance.

Planning the Steps of the Progression

Once you have made your graph showing where you are now and where you hope to go, it is time to plan your training program more carefully. Later in this book you will see training patterns followed by champion runners at different distances. You can use them or modify them to meet your personal training needs. For the off-season or pre-season (before our races begin), Oregon uses a 21-day pattern. For the competitive season, Oregon uses a 14-day pattern, with a more specialized 10-day pattern leading to the most important competitions, such as conference and national championships.

At the end of each pattern or cycle we have either a time trial or a race, which allows us to see whether the runner is progressing. The times are marked on our performance graph, which shows us if any changes in training are needed. For example, if the runner cannot run the trial distance at the Date Pace he has been following in training, the Date Pace will remain the same for the next 21-day training pattern.

The regular time trials calling for gradual improvement in pace during the off-season bring you to goal pace in a predictable manner that minimizes stress. The time trials also callous you to the racing distance. You will not find a race unusually difficult or long when the racing season arrives, because you will have run the race a number of times already.

How Much Training Do You Need?

For most runners, the critical question is not how much they should increase their training, but rather when and how much they should cut it back. A hard/easy pattern is recommended to allow recovery from the hard training days. Only a few runners can train hard for several days in a row on a regular basis with just a single day's recovery. In fact, many runners need two easy days for every hard day of training. You will have to experiment to find out how much rest you need between hard workouts.

The hard training days provide the best indication of your ideal training load. If you feel tired before the hard session, you probably need to cut your training load. The easy days should be genuinely easy. Your pulse should remain low (less than 140) throughout the run. This easy run should not be very long; if you begin to feel tired, you should stop. If you are very tired, you may find that you feel like jogging for only 10 minutes or so.

Remember that you will improve only as long as you maintain a moderate training program, allowing your body to recover from the harder training sessions. If you do not recover enough on your easy days to be fresh for the next hard day, you will be more vulnerable to sickness and injury. Learn to listen to your body and it will tell you whether it is getting enough rest.

When and How Much Should You Increase Your Training Load?

Your overall training load should be increased very gradually. If, for example, you averaged 30 miles a week in training last year, you should not plan to go to 60 miles a week this year. In the early stages of training, you may be able to increase your mileage rapidly as you get into shape; however, once you reach a certain mileage level in training (for example, 40 to 60 miles per week), you should be very cautious about further increases.

Leg injuries such as stress fractures are a common result of overtraining, especially when you try to train at high mileage levels. Injuries can start as nagging pains that upset your workouts. The best way to increase your overall training mileage is in very gradual doses, such as a 10-mile increase in one week, followed by a decrease the next week.

After your highest mileage week, you should back off for the next week or two. The cutback in training gives your body a chance to tell you if the stress of the hard week was too much. A feeling of fatigue from overtraining can be the first signal of impending injury. The extra rest will let your body recover, and any minor aches or pains will either go away or stand out as something other than general fatigue.

Generally, you should only increase your average weekly mileage by about 10 miles per week per year. If you averaged 70 miles a week last year, 80 miles per week is a sound goal for the next year.

Many of Oregon's sub-four-minute milers have averaged 60 miles per week in training. Of course they were talented, but the principle holds. Extremely punishing training is not necessary for successful running. Moderation and gradual progress will improve your chances for success.

What To Do When You Reach Your Goal

What do you do when you reach your goal? Set a higher goal.

If you have reasonable goals and plan your training program carefully, eventually you will reach them. Once you reach those goals, it's time to restart the process of goal-setting. If you have met your goals and you're near the end of a racing season, you should elevate your sights a bit. If the season is over, start planning for next year. Look at what you have accomplished and study your training records to see how you accomplished it.

When the racing season is over, give yourself a vacation. Get involved in some of the activities you could not enjoy while training and racing. If you want to run regularly, just take easy, comfortable runs; do not make them training sessions.

Taking off from running for a few weeks or a month will be a refreshing change. You'll feel ready to return to training with enthusiasm, and you'll look forward to next year's races and goals. Be sure to begin your training at a reduced level. You are starting a new year, not trying to pick up at exactly the same level where you ended the season. Enjoy yourself, start a little higher up the ladder than you started last year, and climb higher than before.

Figure 2: Performance Graph (By Time)

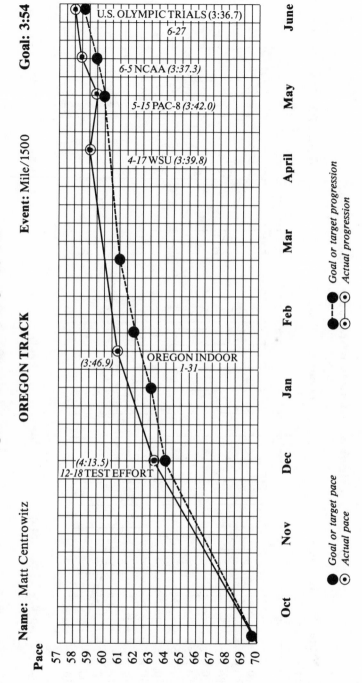

Name: Matt Centrowitz   OREGON TRACK   Event: Mile/1500   Goal: 3:54

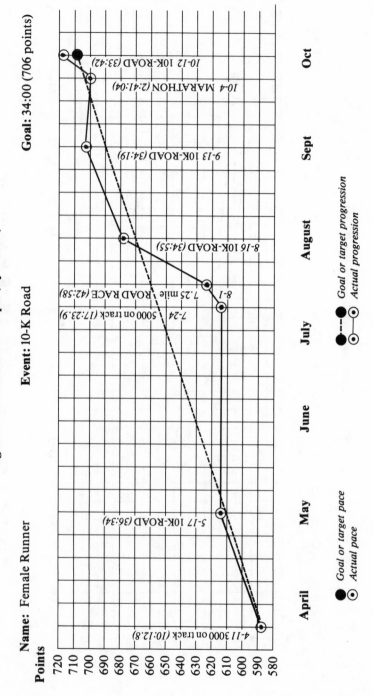

Figure 3: Performance Graph (By Points)

Name: Female Runner   **Event:** 10-K Road   **Goal:** 34:00 (706 points)

Points

720
710
700
690
680
670
660
650
640
630
620
610
600
590
580

April   May   June   July   August   Sept   Oct

4-11 3000 on track (10:12.8)

5-17 10K-ROAD (36:34)

7-24 5000 on track (17:23.9)

8-1 7.25 mile ROAD RACE (42:58)

8-16 10K-ROAD (34:55)

9-13 10K-ROAD (34:19)

10-4 MARATHON (2:41:04)

10-12 10K-ROAD (33:42)

● Goal or target pace   ●—— Goal or target progression
⊙ Actual pace   ⊙—— Actual progression

4. Non-Running Preparation: Icing on the Cake

REST AND DIET

Rest and diet are what we call "common sense training topics." Any athlete in serious training will need a lot of rest. Most distance runners will sleep eight to 10 hours a night, if they can. Getting enough sleep can be a problem for athletes in school, because study time often extends well into the evening.

Ideally, an athlete in training should try to get 10 hours of sleep each night. Consistency is as important in your resting habits as in your training habits. Oregon runners are even encouraged to take a nap in the afternoon. A lack of sleep the night before a race will rarely affect your performance, but consistently poor sleep will. Poor sleeping habits will hurt your racing just as much as poor training habits or overtraining.

Despite the volumes of information on nutrition and diet, the best diet for you is one that you are already accustomed to — just eat in moderation. Avoiding overeating will do more good than trying to adapt to the latest fad diet that supposedly gives you extra energy.

Most runners will get the vitamins and minerals they need through their normal diet. If you are not sure whether your diet has all the essential vitamins and minerals, take a vitamin/mineral supplement. Water-soluble vitamins your body does not use will be excreted naturally, so there is no harm in it. Women runners should check with their doctors about taking iron and calcium supplements, which are useful (often vital) to the female runner's success.

The prerace meal should be eaten at least five hours before the race and consist of foods easily digested and high in carbohydrates. Many Oregon runners prefer toast, a bowl of peaches, and tea or coffee. This meal gives enough nourishment so that hunger will not be a problem before the race, yet the stomach will be empty by race time. For races lasting more than two hours, many runners will have a large helping of spaghetti or pasta the evening before the race.

PREVENTING INJURIES

When you are trying to reach a peak for competition, you should avoid participating in unfamiliar activities. A frequent cause of non-running injuries to runners is pick-up or intramural basketball and touch football. Just use good judgment before you try other activities.

Never try to train through an injury. It is the best way to injure yourself again, you'll slow your recovery and you can make your current injury worse. For most running-related injuries, the best treatment is rest. This is where "running streaks" (not missing running for many days or years in a row) can be harmful. Don't risk further injury by running hurt just to keep a streak going.

When you can walk and jog without favoring the injury, you can begin to train again. Determine your condition at that point and start to progress. Just as you don't want to train while injured, you should not try to make up missed training too quickly.

The most common interruption to training is the cold. A cold runs its course in about 10 days. You should not try to continue training hard while you have a cold. You should run gently or rest, depending on how bad the cold is. If you keep training at a high level, you are more likely to cause the cold to settle deeper into your chest. The risk of longer-lasting secondary infections is also greatly increased.

This is where knowing how to "read" your body is very important. When you feel you are tired or getting "run down," you should cut back on your training, run shorter and slower workouts, or even take a complete rest. Training when the body is physically "down" only weakens it. An occasional two- or three-day break from training can help a runner, especially one who is tired or sick.

Most injuries of the foot, ankle, leg, knee and hip result from poor running technique, rather than from accidents. The greatest stresses are created by overstriding and/or running on the balls of the feet, like a sprinter. Runners' feet land one of three ways: heel-first, then rolling forward across the bottom of the foot; flat-footed; or on the ball of the foot. If you cannot stop running on your toes, you are less likely to become injured if you run on soft surfaces. Otherwise, shinsplints and stress fractures to the lower leg are possible.

Good shoes are important in preventing injury. Rather than recommend specific shoes in a market which is rapidly changing, we will look at the characteristics of a good running shoe. Look for these points: 1) The midsole and heel wedge should be soft enough to cushion and protect the foot, particularly the ball of the foot, and the sole should be made of a rubber that will last for many miles. If the sole is too stiff, like a basketball shoe, it will not permit the flexibility your foot needs for proper running action. 2) The shoe should have a good arch support, and a heel raised about a half-inch higher than the ball of the foot, to prevent overstretching or straining the Achilles tendon and the calf muscles. 3) A wide base at the heel will help stabilize your foot against too much side-to-side twisting when you run. 4) The shoe should fit well, but allow room for your toes to move. Remember that because a specific model is perfect for a friend, it will not necessarily be right for you. Compare the comfort of a number of available models before picking a shoe.

Shinsplints and Posture

Shinsplints (soreness along the front or sides of the lower leg) is perhaps the most common running injury. Among its causes are poor shoes and running too much on hard surfaces. You can ice the soreness to reduce inflammation and promote healing. Stretching exercises may help prevent shinsplints. Here's one exercise: Sit with one leg crossed over the other and use your hands to move your raised foot through and slightly beyond its normal range of motion (up and down, as well as to the sides), working on each foot for one minute a day.

Your running posture is important in preventing injuries, as well as for efficiency. You should try to "run tall," keeping your upper body erect and lifting your chest. Your pelvis should be tipped a bit forward and up to improve the efficiency of your leg movements.

This position can be simulated and your position improved by backing against a wall, tightening your abdominal muscles and trying to touch the small of your back to the wall. An exercise for this position can be performed by lying on your back. Assume the position for a straight back, then slowly lift your legs off the floor and hold them off for a count of 30 or for 30 seconds. At first you should do this with your legs bent at the knees, which is easier. As you become stronger, you should perform the exercise with your legs straight. However, if you also do sit-ups, always perform them with your legs bent, because straight-legged sit-ups can strain the muscles of the lower back.

A good program of conditioning will help considerably in preventing injuries. Generally, the better your overall condition, the better your chances of avoiding injury.

STRENGTH CONDITIONING

For our purposes, conditioning falls into three categories: strength, flexibility and running. Runners too often overlook strength and flexibility in their running. Runners may have weak upper bodies without special training. A distance runner does not want a competitive weightlifter's upper body, but strength is a big help in running faster. And flexibility can develop a more efficient running technique.

At Oregon, strength exercises are done with both free weights and Nautilus machines. Most of the runners' weight training is done with light weights, using many repetitions to emphasize endurance. In the off-season, Oregon runners lift weights three days a week, reducing to two days a week during the racing season. Here is a simple list of exercises for the typical runner using free weights:

Exercise	Sets	Reps	Days	Comments
Dumbbell Fly	1	25	M-W-F	10 lb. weights
Leg Press	3	50	W	Add weight each month
Breathing Dead Lift	3	10	M-W-F	As heavy as you can position
Seated Press	3	8	W	Start with ¼ body weight
Bench Press	3	8	M	Start with ¼ body weight
Pulldowns	3	8	F	
Rope Climb	2		M-W-F	Build up to using no legs
Sit-ups	4	25	M-W-F	
Straight Arm Pullover	3	8	W-F	Increase monthly until 40 lbs.

This program can be varied for your needs. Padded training benches can be used to help with other exercises (with and without added weights), such as back extensions, incline and decline sit-ups, hip and back flexes, leg extensions and single and double leg curls. Running in place with hand weights is useful for working on style. Stand in place while swinging the arms through the normal range of running motions. Our more recent exercise list includes the following exercises:

Arm curls on Nautilus
Pullovers on Nautilus
Single and double leg curls on weight bench
Leg extensions on weight bench
Incline sit-ups on bench
Decline sit-ups on bench
Back extensions on a bench
Hip and back flexes on bench
Hip flexors while hanging from a stall bar
Form running (moving arms only) with hand weights
Front lateral raises with hand weights
   Breathe in on raising the weights in front
   Breathe out while lowering the weights to the side

Diaphragm exercise
Deep inhales while holding a barbell down at arm's length

Calf raises: three positions for the feet
Toes pointed straight forward, toes pointed inward, and toes pointed outward

Abductor-adductor stretching
Seated position on the floor, legs split toward the sides

You can find many helpful books with more details on strength training programs, both with free weights and for Nautilus machines. Strength is important to successful running; a well-rounded training program will not overlook it.

FLEXIBILITY CONDITIONING: JUST ENOUGH

Stretching exercises will help to prevent injuries in your running and racing, and allow you to use more efficient running technique. Try to do 15 to 20 minutes of stretching or flexibility work both before and after running. Oregon runners use 10 different exercises, aimed at stretching different muscles or muscle combinations. They want to develop useful flexibility, not train to perform unusual exercises. Moderation is important in the choice and application of stretching exercises. When you try a new exercise, do it carefully and for a short time. The effects of overstretching or other training exercises will not always show up on the same day the training occurs. With each exercise, you should gradually stretch the muscle, then hold the position, rather than make any quick yanking or bouncing movements.

The exercises to use or areas to stretch follow:

Gluteals: Seated, extend one leg straight forward and hold the other knee to your chest, with the foot of your bent leg placed on the floor on the opposite side of the lowered thigh. Reverse the leg positions to stretch the other leg.

Hamstrings and quads: Lying down, raise one knee to your chest, then lower it and raise the other knee to your chest.

Groin and hamstrings: Hanging from a bar, raise your legs in a split position upward and toward the sides, trying to raise the feet as high as your waist.

Lower back: Seated, with your legs foward, lean as far forward as you can, stretching your hands toward your feet.

Hamstrings and gluteals: Standing in a crouch on a bench or stair, with your knees bent and your fingertips holding the bottom of the bench or stair edge, gradually straighten your legs as much as you can.

Split stretch: Standing with one foot directly in front of the other, gradually stretch your feet as far apart as possible, putting your hands on the floor at your sides for balance.

The Bridge: Start by lying on your back and then lifting yourself off the ground by arching your back, supporting yourself with your hands and feet.

Hurdle stretch: Sit with one leg straight to the front, and the other leg to the side with a knee bent toward the rear; you can stretch both forward and backward.

Calf stretches: 1) Leaning forward, support your hands and feet on the floor with your hips raised high in the air, alternately stretching one calf while bending the other leg forward at the knee. 2) Lean forward against a wall. Extend a leg behind you and stretch the calf muscle.

Standing hip flex: Stand sideways to the wall, hands at your sides. Now bend your hip sideways toward the wall.

Remember not to get too wrapped up in your stretching program. Overstretching will detract from, rather than add to, your running.

CIRCUIT TRAINING FOR BASE CONDITIONING

Circuit training is a good way to improve your physical condition, strength and flexibility. It is most popular in European systems of training, but has many virtues as an adjunct to your training program. Circuit training was developed as a way to maintain all-around fitness during the harsh winter months in areas with limited indoor exercise facilities. Essentially, it combines calisthenics and weight training exercises performed at varying speeds. Participants move from one exercise station to the next, with the entire circuit timed from start to finish. It combines both strength and flexibility training with cardio-respiratory training.

Because winters in Eugene, Ore., are relatively mild, though wet, Oregon runners do their circuit training outdoors at the mile-long Amazon Trail public jogging loop about a mile from campus. Their circuit training is based on a program developed by Luis de Oliveira, the Brazilian coach of 800-meter star Joaquim Cruz.

Our circuit is a 1000-meter loop with nine exercise stations, each station positioned 100 meters from the next. Before beginning circuit training, the runners spend a day going over the different exercises and learning how they are performed. Then we test each runner to see how many repetitions of each exercise can be performed within a time limit.

The exercise stations follow an easy/medium/hard pattern. In the preliminary tests, the exercises for the easy stations are performed for 60 seconds, and the medium stations for 30 seconds. At the hard stations, the runners do as many repetitions as they can, until it's noticeably more difficult to continue. There is no time limit on the hard exercise stations, as opposed to the easy and medium stations.

Each runner performs half as many repetitions at each station as he was able to perform in the test. Each 100 meters between stations, and from station 9 to the end of the kilometer, is run as quickly as possible. The station (4, 7, and Finish) following the hard station always begins with a 90-second rest, before the easy exercise is performed. The stations and exercises we perform are similar to those found at many Parcourses, so you can follow along. The exercises follow:

Station 1: Trunk side flex (Easy). Test time: 60 seconds. Standing with your feet spread slightly, reach for your toes with your hands, then sweep your hands to one side, going down and then to the other side on the next repetition. The movement should be smooth and fluid, not jerky or bouncing. Now run 100 meters to the next station.

Station 2: Elevated skip (Medium). Test time: 30 seconds. Alternately kick up one leg, then the other, a bit like lifting your leg to clear a hurdle, except the leg is kept as straight as possible at the knee. As your leg is kicked up, lean foward toward your knee to your chest, clapping your hands under your raised leg. This is done by bouncing or springing off the supporting leg. Do not try to move too quickly and risk pulling a muscle. Run to the next station.

Station 3: Leg flex and jump (Hard). No time limit. Begin by crouching until your knees are at a 90-degree angle and your thighs are parallel to the ground. Swing your arms up and jump as high as you can. This bouncing, flexing exercise improves both leg spring and strength. Run 100 meters to the next station.

Station 4: Jumping jacks (Easy). Test time: 60 seconds. This station begins with a 90-second rest, to allow recovery from the hard station and 100-meter run. Do jumping jacks (or side-straddle hops) for 60 seconds, stretching your arms above your head. Run to the next station.

Station 5: Kicking the moon (Medium). Test time: 30 seconds. Beginning in the push-up position with your arms extended, raise your hips and swing one leg to the side and forward, with your relatively straight knee moving toward your arm; then return the leg to the starting position. Do not stop in a support position while switching from one leg to the other. It is a non-stop exercise moving back and forth from side to side. This will require balance and hip rotation, so be careful of your balance and do not try to move too quickly. Run to the next station.

Station 6: Shuttle run (Hard). Make three markers or points 10 meters apart. The shuttle run goes from the start to the first marker, then returns to the start. Next it goes from the start to the last marker and back to the start. One repetition is one short shuttle and one long shuttle. At each turning point, you will touch the ground or line with your hand. Run to the next station.

Station 7: Hip twists — trunk rotations (Easy). Test time: 60 seconds. This station begins with a 90-second rest. Standing

Figure 4: *Circuit Training Record*

Time	Names	*1) Jim Hill*		*2) Don Clary*		*3) Alberto Salazar*	
	Stations	Max.	50%	Max.	50%	Max.	50%
60 sec.	1. Trunk Flex	50	25				
30 sec.	2. Elevated Skip	44	22				
MAX.	3. Leg Flex and Jump	30	15				
60 sec.	4. Jumping Jacks	70	35				
30 sec.	5. Kicking the Moon	30	15				
MAX.	6. Shuttle Run	10	5				
60 sec.	7. Hip	80	40				
30 sec.	8. High Knees	50	25				
MAX.	9. Burpees	20	10				

Goal Time

Goal Time
(continued)

1) Jim Hill	*2) Don Clary*
Date:	Date:
Time:	Time:
Date:	Date:
Time:	Time:
Date:	Date:
Time:	Time:
Date:	Date:
Time:	Time:
Date:	Date:
Time:	Time:
Date:	Date:
Time:	Time:
Date:	Date:
Time:	Time:
Date:	Date:
Time:	Time:
Date:	Date:
Time:	Time:
Date:	Date:
Time:	Time:
Date:	Date:
Time:	Time:

with your arms out to your sides, swing them around as far as you can, first clockwise, then counterclockwise, to complete one repetition. At the same time, you will leave the ground to rotate your legs and hips in the opposite direction to your arms. Run to the next station.

Station 8: High knee exercise (Medium). Test time: 30 seconds. As you run in place, simulate a sprinter's running technique, but exaggerate the knee lift and arm swing. The emphasis should be on technique; bounce off your toes as you lift each knee. Two simple warnings should be followed here: 1) Do not try to see how fast you can perform the drill, because there is strong risk of a muscle pull, and 2) run in place on a soft surface, to help ease the stress on your legs. Run to the next station.

Station 9: Burpees (Hard). Each repetition gets four counts. 1) From a standing position, squat down and put your hands on the ground in preparation for a push-up. 2) Thrust your legs behind you, putting yourself into a push-up position. 3) Return to position one, with your legs beneath your body and your hands on the ground. 4) Swing your arms forward and up, jumping as high as you can. Run to the end of the circuit.

At the end of the circuit, rest for three minutes. Then run the 1000-meter circuit without stopping, after which you will rest for another three minutes. You may want to jog during the three-minute rest. A five- or ten-kilometer runner or marathoner might run 1500 meters or one mile, instead of one kilometer (1000 meters).

The initial time is recorded for each runner. That time is multiplied by three to give a goal time for performing three loops of the circuit in one session later in the training year. Remember to add in the three-minute recoveries after the first two sets. For example, if you run the circuit once in 20 minutes (to the end of your 1000-meter run), your goal time for three complete circuits would be 2×23 minutes (to allow the extra 3:00 before starting again), plus 20 minutes, or a total of 66 minutes.

You will begin training by running the circuit a single time, but as your strength increases, you will run it twice, and eventually you will run it three times. About once a month you should retest your performance in each of the skills, then raise the number of repetitions you do at each station to 50 percent of the new maximum-tested levels as your condition improves.

The circuit provides all-around conditioning, helping with strength, flexibility, coordination and cardio-respiratory endurance. When you can go through the circuit three times, you've had a good hour workout, including running 30×100-meter accelerations and 3×1000-meter intervals.

TRAINING THE MIND

Not all of a champion's training is concerned with the physical. The mental aspects are just as important as physical conditioning and strength. A champion athlete is as mentally tough as he is physically tough. The next chapter discusses the non-physical aspects of a runner's preparations.

5. The Inner Runner: Toughness for the Mind

Every person has a certain amount of athletic talent and potential. Part of this is genetic — a gift from your parents. Another part is the improvement you have made through your training program. Regardless of the inherited and developed levels of ability, the "best" person will not always win the race.

Why? Scientists suggest that 80 percent of your physical potential is inherited. The remaining 20 percent comes from the mind. We need to consider seriously the mental side of training and racing, because running is an act of the will as much as of the body.

You have heard many times that one athlete or another is a very determined competitor. That description is moving away from the physical component of running to the mental component. To run your best, you must use your mind as well as your body. The will to succeed is as important as the physical ability to succeed. Several subjective factors are involved in that "will to succeed."

SELF-DISCIPLINE

One of the qualities that separates one person from another is self-discipline. Some people are very self-disciplined, but others have trouble getting out of bed in the morning, much less going for a run. However, self-discipline is not a quality that is inherited or has limits placed upon it. We each have as much self-discipline as we choose to have; there is no limit.

Self-discipline can be developed to become a major factor in a race. A less-talented runner can train to higher levels and defeat an opponent who has more talent, but lacks the self-discipline to reach his potential.

One example of a person with self-discipline is Lars Kaupang, a Norwegian student who came to Oregon as a 4:17 miler. He had a normal quota of inherited talent, but also a great capacity for self-discipline. He improved gradually while at Oregon, eventually breaking four minutes for a mile. In 1976 he ran the 1500 meters in 3:37.4. When a runner is self-disciplined, no coach can predict what levels of performance he will eventually reach.

An example of self-discipline in a more talented athlete is Alberto Salazar's training for the 1980 U.S. Olympic Trials. Injuries had hurt his spring training and racing so that he was unable to run well for many weeks. Instead, he worked hard on an exercise bicycle and in the swimming pool, training at a high level in whatever way he could. Able to run again for four weeks before the Trials, he found that he had maintained his conditioning so well that he was able to make the Olympic Team and run within four seconds of his personal best for 10,000 meters.

Self-discipline is best attained early in life. The discipline your parents imposed on you when you were younger could be good training for the later years, when your discipline is self-imposed. Success will not be possible without self-discipline, no matter how much talent, education, or luck you have.

Mental Toughness

Mental toughness is easier to point out than it is to define. It is a quality found in the person who competes to the best of his ability regardless of the race conditions. You may not win the race, but competing to the best of your ability is not defined in those terms. Regardless of an athlete's mental toughness, only one person can be the winner. If you have performed to the best of your ability, regardless of the conditions, then — win or lose — you are a champion.

A good running program should develop mental toughness. In training it is developed by occasionally challenging the runner with workouts designed to test his physical and mental capacity fully. The training session must approach the athlete's limit, but it should not go past that limit, as we discussed with the callousing effect. Mental toughness is developed by accomplishment, not failure.

The easiest way is not always the best way to promote mental toughness. Primitive training facilities, adverse weather and other obstacles can cultivate mental toughness. A runner must face tough situations in training to cope effectively with tough situations in competition.

An example of mental toughness is Bill McChesney's 5000-meter race in the 1980 U.S. Olympic Trials. He had already shown his aggressive running in taking third at the NCAA meet, but his relatively slow PR made him a longshot for the Trials races. He decided to try to "steal" the race, sprinting to the front with a mile to go and opening a large lead. His mental toughness allowed him to take a risky chance and to hold on to make the U.S. Olympic Team with a PR. Running in Europe in 1980, he eventually cut almost 25 seconds off his 1979 PR, finishing the year as the sixth-fastest performer in the world.

Another factor in mental toughness is what we call the "inverted pyramid." A runner who has been successful finds that he is in a position where people expect him to be tough and to compete successfully, regardless of the circumstances. Because of the expectations placed upon him, he has to be tough. The late Steve Prefontaine said that what his fans expected from him helped to sustain him in races that were so tough he was ready to break. A runner who does not have high expectations placed upon him finds it easier to quit or back off when the pace gets tough. Once he does this, it will be easier to quit or back off the next time.

Winning Attitude

To be a winner, you must think of yourself as a winner. Self-confidence is a necessity. It can come partly from confidence in your coach and your program. Indeed, one of the greatest aids to success you can have is a coach and running program in which you have complete faith. A trademark of great coaches is their ability to gain the respect and confidence of the men and women they are training.

As a person matures, he naturally gains a certain degree of self-confidence. Experience soon teaches a runner his strengths and weaknesses. We gain confidence by doing what we know we can do well, and by avoiding doing things we know are beyond our capabilities.

Youth does not have this advantage. To develop a winner's attitude, you should allow room for achievable success. Competitions should be fun-time activities. If the goal is to participate and to have fun, everyone can be a winner, regardless of his finishing place.

All young runners should begin as sprinters. Knowing how to sprint is a valuable tool in later years when many runners turn to the distance events. A structured running program should not begin until at least the junior high school years, as a runner enters his teens.

Do not be afraid to daydream about running. You have to picture yourself as a winner. When I was training for the 1964 Tokyo Olympics, I ran that race at least 10,000 times in my mind. Every time I ran the race it was under different circumstances with varying conditions and tactics thrown in. Only one thing never changed: I always won the race! However, dreaming is a dead end unless it is blended with self-discipline and a willingness to push yourself with hard work.

A program that enhances a winning attitude is one that does not put undue pressure on finishing first. It's a mistake for a coach to tell a runner he has to win, or for the runner to put undue pressure on himself by believing he must win.

Oregon runners are asked to compete to the best of their ability under all circumstances. Maximum effort can become a habit. Runners must have faith that their coach will not enter them in events for which they are ill-prepared. Achievement and satisfaction are not exclusively for the runner who finishes first. They are shared by anyone who knows deep down inside that he gets the maximum possible from his abilities.

As coaches, we do not want to try to pinpoint the blend of ingredients for greatness. Someone may have a combination of psychological and physiological tests for greatness someday, though that day has not arrived. We have seen greatness, though: in the eyes of Steve Prefontaine at the starting line, or in the concentration of Mac Wilkins preparing for a discus throw. Anyone can see it in the stubbornness of a child at play who loses, but comes back again and again until he finally succeeds.

You can better achieve your potential by mapping out a plan. The guidelines for coach and athlete include:

1. demanding and expecting discipline
2. allowing for accomplishment through progression
3. allowing for individual differences in training
4. using common sense
5. developing a callousing effect for physical progression and mental preparation
6. allowing for and utilizing feedback from runners
7. challenging yourself to the limit
8. emphasizing participation, rather than "coming in first"

You can speed up your development of those championship qualities in a number of ways. Remember to:

1) Be patient.
2) Be realistic.
3) Be goal-oriented.
4) Be persistent.
5) Be consistent.
6) Use common sense.
7) Complete workouts, even if adjustments have to be made.
8) Ask questions.
9) Listen.
10) Discipline yourself in all phases of life.

Use your mind to help yourself become a champion in life!

6. Using a Training Diary

You've probably always read that all serious runners should keep a training diary. We agree. The idea of a training diary raises two questions: Why should I keep a diary, and what should I put in it? Let's look at both questions.

Why Keep a Training Diary?

Keeping good records can show you where you went wrong in training, how that unexpected injury came about, and what training plan would work best for you.

You won't see a subhead for "Injuries started today" or "Poor workout choice" or anything so obvious. Instead, you'll have a record of what you did, the conditions under which you did your workout and how your body reacted to or was affected by it. The major training questions are answered when you study your records, weeks, months or even years later and look for patterns of success or failure.

One of the "secrets" of the East German success in track and field is that they try to recreate the conditions of success. For example, they test athletes' blood to learn as much as possible about their physiology so they can compare it to test results made when the athlete had his previous best performance. They then try to train the athlete so that the same blood values are recreated for the next major competition. A training diary will show you how you prepared for a race, and what the results were for that preparation.

If you have not been racing well, compare your recent training to your training when you were doing better. How has your training changed? Are you training longer or more intensely? Are you racing more often? Are you allowing fewer recovery days? Has your weight risen or dropped very much? Many factors can affect training and racing, and only with a thorough record of your training can you hope to understand how your body reacts to the stresses you place upon it.

What Should Be Included in a Training Diary?

Your training diary should include any factors that affect the quality of your training or racing. Various training diaries are sold at book stores and running shops, if you want to buy one, or you can make your own.

A typical retail diary may have a week's workouts on two facing pages of the notebook, so you can look at a week of training at a time. Each day has a separate section, with a space for the date, a blank section for the workout to be recorded, and places to record the pace, the weather, distance covered in the workout, and the total mileage (to that point) for the week. Space may also be given for you to record your daily weight and morning pulse. An example is shown on page 65.

Most diaries sold are oriented toward distance running and distance (rather than interval or fartlek) workouts. However, you can easily record other information in your own way in one of those books. Runner's World Books, for example, sells a training diary that includes sections for recording your race results, the progress of your PRs (personal records) at several distances, various training records (longest run, and such), records for any loops or circuits you may run, and several graphs. All of those things can be helpful to a runner, and, if nothing else, fascinating reading.

Here are some examples of factors you might like to include in your personal training diary:

Date.

Resting pulse. What was your pulse that morning? Your pulse is usually taken for one minute after awakening, but before sitting up or getting out of bed. Your pulse can indicate your general condition and fatigue level. If your pulse is 10 beats or more above normal, you may need more rest, rather than more training.

There is no "right" pulse rate for success. Some mediocre runners have very low pulse rates, and some excellent ones do not. Jim Ryun's resting pulse was usually about 70.

But the pulse is definitely a very useful indicator of the intensity of a workout. You can learn to judge your pulse rate while running, which helps in developing a good sense of proper pacing effort.

Sleep and naps. How long did you sleep the night before? Recording the time to bed and time of rising gives a general idea of resting time. You should also note how well you slept. Poor sleep may indicate other problems, but it is a common symptom of overtraining or overfatigue.

You might also want to include nap times, if you take naps. Many serious runners will sleep from eight to 10 hours a night, and others will sleep even more than that while training at a high level.

Food, if unusual. Did you eat anything that you don't usually eat? When you first begin to train and race, you can benefit by recording everything you eat for a while. You may learn if any foods cause problems for your running or racing. Some people can eat anything, whereas others have very sensitive stomachs. There is no one "correct" or "perfect" training or racing diet. Carbohydrate loading gets a lot of press, but is a factor (if at all) only in races of about two hours or longer.

Weather. The conditions during each workout. You might include the temperature, humidity, and wind conditions (speed and direction, plus chill factor in winter).

Training conditions. Terrain you ran on. Was the ground dry, wet or muddy? Were running conditions fast or slow? Did anything else about the conditions affect your training session?

The workout. What did you do? Do not record what you wanted to do, or the times you would have run in better conditions. Just as you record the real training conditions, record the workout session as accurately as you can. Record what you did for a warmup and cooldown. If you use the same warmup and cooldown for every session, make note of it somewhere in your records as your usual pattern. Then just list "warmup" and "cooldown," unless you do something different. Always list any stretching exercises you try that are out of the ordinary, just as you should record any slips, overstretching, turning an ankle or a fall.

If you took a long run, give the approximate distance and the estimated pace or total time for the run.

If you ran intervals, give the number and distance, the times or average times, and the recovery distance and/or time.

If you ran a fartlek session, give the approximate distance and total time, along with the effort level. Include the number and/or approximate length of the faster parts of the run.

Race or time trial results. How did you do? For a race, record splits, if you know them, and details about how you ran the race — tactics, pacing variations, course oddities and such. This is a good place for notes on things you want to try the next time.

Physical effect of session. How did the workout feel? How hard did the session seem to you, and how did you feel before, during and after the session? Noted track expert and runner Fred Wilt used a rating scale (1 to 9) for how he felt before the session, in the middle of a workout, and after he was finished. Or, you can jot down your feelings, such as "tired before workout" or "felt very good today."

Any problems (before, during or after the workout). Was anything wrong? You should record any injuries or soreness, in case you have any physical problems later. These notes, along with records of your fatigue levels, can give vital clues to the onset of injuries. And make note of anything else that impedes the workout, such as running too soon after eating or rushing to start or finish the workout.

You should include anything that happens but is not normal or usual in your training sessions.

Body weight. How much did you weigh? Record your weight without clothes both before and after the workout.

Mileage of workout session (and day, if you ran more than once). Keep a cumulative total for each week. However, do not let yourself become obsessed by mileage totals.

You may think of other items you would like to include in your training record. Look at your training record as a guide to help you avoid making the same mistakes again. It indicates how you succeeded and how you failed. This makes it easier for you to get the results you want in the future.

A Typical Training Diary

Sunday   **Date:**   / /

Pace	**Weather**	**Distance**	**Week Total**

Summary:

Week total:		**Longest run:**	**Shortest run:**
Average run:		**Month total:**	**Year total:**

Daily Weight: **Morning pulse:**

Sun	Thurs	Sun	Thurs
Mon	Fri	Mon	Fri
Tues	Sat	Tues	Sat
Wed		Wed	

A Possible Workout Record

1) Day: Tuesday   Date: 4/17/84   **2) Morning pulse:** 42
3) Sleep: from 10:15 p.m. to 8:30 a.m.   **Total:** 10¼ hours
   Naps: 45 min. after lunch
4) Food: Chili overdose at lunch

5) Weather: Temp: 64 °F **Hum:** 55% **Wind:** 6 mph, SW
Notes: Head wind off last turn; weather felt nice.

6) Training location and conditions: Track — dry, fairly fast

7) Workout: [or, **8) Race or Trial results:**]
Warmup [usual]
10 × 330 in 54 with 110 jogs — avg. 53.6
20 min. easy run — 2¼ miles through park on grass
6 × 330 cutdowns with 110 jogs — 56, 55.5, 53.5, 54.0, 53.5
  52.8
Cooldown — 10 min. jog in cemetery — quiet

9) Fatigue level [1-9]: **Before** 2 **Mid** 4 **After** 5

10) Any problems? Felt the chili during the cut-downs

11) Body weight: Before w/o: 145 lbs. After w/o: 144 lbs.

12) Total miles: 9½ **Daily total:** 13 **Week total:** 31

7. A Training Program for the New Runner

Before you can race, you must be able to run; before you can run, you must be able to jog. This 10-week program is for the person who is new to jogging or running, but is in good health. The program leads you to the status of regular jogger, in this case a 20-minute-per-day jogger. When you can jog 20 minutes per day comfortably, you will be ready to try the low-mileage — but more intense — runner's training programs. After the 10-week program we will introduce a training program for the 1500-meter or one-mile run and for the 5000- to 10,000-meter track or road races.

Rather than run on a track for a certain distance, find a park or an area you would like to run in. You needn't concern yourself with distance in yards and miles. Just count your steps, one count for every time your right foot touches the ground, using your fingers to count by tens. You should begin by mixing jogging with walking, gradually increasing the time spent jogging.

As your condition improves, change the walks taken on your "easy" days to jogs. At the end of 10 weeks, you should be able to jog for 20 minutes a day. Monday, Wednesday and Friday will be your "easy" days, and Tuesday, Thursday and Saturday will be your "hard" days. Sunday should be taken up by some other activity; although it is a rest day, it is not an inactive day.

Ten Week Pre-Training Program
Week 1

Monday: Jog for 10 counts of your right foot, then walk for 20 counts of your right foot. Repeat the process for 20 minutes.

Tuesday: Walk for 20 minutes.

Wednesday: Jog for 20 counts of your right foot, then walk for 20 counts of your right foot. Repeat the process for 20 minutes.

Thursday: Walk for 20 minutes.

Friday: Jog for 20 counts of your right foot, then walk for 10 counts of your right foot. Repeat the process for 20 minutes.

Saturday: Walk for 20 minutes.

Week 2

Monday: Jog for 20 counts of your right foot, then walk for 20 counts of your right foot. Repeat the process for 20 minutes.

Tuesday: Walk for 5 minutes; jog for 5 minutes using the count system (jog for 50 counts, then walk for 50 counts, repeating the sequence for 5 minutes); walk for 5 minutes, then jog for 5 minutes using the count system (jog 50, walk 50).

Wednesday: Jog for 30 counts of your right foot, then walk for 20 counts of your right foot. Repeat the process for 20 minutes.

Thursday: Walk for 5 minutes, then jog for 5 minutes using the count system (jog for 50 counts, then walk for 50 counts, repeating the sequence for 5 minutes); walk for 5 minutes, then jog for 5 minutes using the count system (jog 50, walk 50).

Friday: Jog for 40 counts of your right foot, then walk for 20 counts of your right foot. Repeat the process for 20 minutes.

Saturday: Walk for 5 minutes, then jog for 5 minutes using the count system (jog for 50 counts,

(continued)	then walk for 50 counts, repeating the sequence for 5 minutes); walk 5 minutes, then jog for 5 minutes using the count system (jog 50, walk 50).

Week 3

Monday:	Jog for 30 counts of your right foot, then walk for 20 counts of your right foot. Repeat the process for 20 minutes.
Tuesday:	Walk briskly for 5 minutes, then jog for 5 minutes using the count system (jog for 50 counts, then walk for 40 counts, repeating the sequence for 5 minutes); walk briskly for 5 minutes, then jog for 5 minutes using the count system (jog 50, walk 50).
Wednesday:	Jog for 40 counts of your right foot, then walk for 20 counts of your right foot. Repeat the process for 20 minutes.
Thursday:	Walk briskly for 5 minutes, then jog for 5 minutes using the count system (jog for 50 counts, then walk for 40 counts, repeating the sequence for five minutes); walk briskly for 5 minutes, then jog for 5 minutes using the count system (jog 50, walk 50).
Friday:	Jog for 50 counts of your right foot, then walk for 30 counts of your right foot. Repeat the process for 20 minutes.
Saturday:	Walk briskly for 5 minutes, then jog for 5 minutes using the count system (jog for 50 counts, then walk for 40 counts, repeating the sequence for 5 minutes); walk briskly for 5 minutes, then jog for 5 minutes using the count system (jog 50, walk 50).

Week 4

Monday:	Jog for 40 counts of your right foot, then walk for 20 counts of your right foot. Repeat the process for 20 minutes.
Tuesday:	Walk briskly for 5 minutes, then jog for 5 minutes using the count system (jog for 50 counts, then walk for 30 counts, repeating the

(continued)   sequence for 5 minutes); walk briskly for 5 minutes, then jog for 5 minutes using the count system (jog 50, walk 30).

Wednesday: Jog for 50 counts of your right foot, then walk for 20 counts of your right foot. Repeat the process for 20 minutes.

Thursday: Walk briskly for 5 minutes, then jog for 5 minutes using the count system (jog for 50 counts, then walk for 30 counts, repeating the sequence for five minutes); walk briskly for 5 minutes, then jog for 5 minutes using the count system (jog 50, walk 30).

Friday: Jog for 60 counts of your right foot, then walk for 20 counts of your right foot. Repeat the process for 20 minutes.

Saturday: Walk briskly for 5 minutes, then jog for 5 minutes using the count system (jog for 50 counts, then walk for 30 counts, repeating the sequence for 5 minutes); walk briskly for 5 minutes, then jog for 5 minutes using the count system (jog 50, walk 30).

Week 5

Monday: Jog for 50 counts of your right foot, then walk for 20 counts of your right foot. Repeat the process for 20 minutes.

Tuesday: Walk briskly for 5 minutes, jog at an easy pace for 5 minutes; walk briskly for 5 minutes, then jog at an easy pace for 5 minutes.

Wednesday: Jog for 60 counts of your right foot, then walk for 20 counts of your right foot. Repeat the process for 20 minutes.

Thursday: Walk briskly for 5 minutes, then jog at an easy pace for 5 minutes; walk briskly for 5 minutes, then jog at an easy pace for 5 minutes.

Friday: Jog for 70 counts of your right foot, then walk for 20 counts of your right foot. Repeat the process for 20 minutes.

Saturday: Walk briskly for 5 minutes, jog at an easy pace for 5 minutes; walk briskly for 5 minutes, jog at an easy pace for 5 minutes.

Week 6

Monday: Jog for 70 counts of your right foot, then walk for 20 counts of your right foot. Repeat the process for 20 minutes.

Tuesday: Walk briskly for 5 minutes, jog at a comfortable pace for 5 minutes; walk briskly for 5 minutes, then jog at an easy pace for 5 minutes.

Wednesday: Jog for 80 counts of your right foot, then walk for 20 counts of your right foot. Repeat the process for 20 minutes.

Thursday: Walk briskly for 5 minutes, jog at a comfortable pace for 5 minutes; walk briskly for 5 minutes, then jog at a comfortable pace for 5 minutes.

Friday: Jog for 90 counts of your right foot, then walk for 20 counts of your right foot. Repeat the process for 20 minutes.

Saturday: Walk briskly for 5 minutes, jog at a comfortable pace for 5 minutes; walk briskly for 5 minutes, jog at a comfortable pace for 5 minutes.

Week 7

Monday: Jog for 90 counts of your right foot, then walk for 20 counts of your right foot. Repeat the process for 20 minutes.

Tuesday: Walk for 5 minutes, jog for 5 minutes; walk for 5 minutes, jog for 5 minutes.

Wednesday: Jog for 100 counts of your right foot, then walk for 20 counts of your right foot. Repeat the process for 20 minutes.

Thursday: Walk for 3 minutes, then jog for 7 minutes; walk for 3 minutes, then jog for 7 minutes.

Friday: Jog for 110 counts of your right foot, then walk for 20 counts of your right foot. Repeat the process for 20 minutes.

Saturday:	Walk for 5 minutes, jog for 10 minutes; walk for 5 minutes.

Week 8

Monday:	Jog for 110 counts of your right foot, then walk for 20 counts of your right foot. Repeat the process for 20 minutes.
Tuesday:	Walk for 3 minutes, jog for 7 minutes; walk for 3 minutes, jog for 7 minutes.
Wednesday:	Jog for 120 counts of your right foot, then walk for 20 counts of your right foot. Repeat the process for 20 minutes.
Thursday:	Walk for 5 minutes; jog for 10 minutes; walk for 5 minutes.
Friday:	Jog for 130 counts of your right foot, then walk for 20 counts of your right foot. Repeat the process for 20 minutes.
Saturday:	Walk for 3 minutes; jog for 14 minutes; walk for 3 minutes.

Week 9

Monday:	Jog for 130 counts of your right foot, then walk for 20 counts of your right foot. Repeat the process for 20 minutes.
Tuesday:	Walk for 5 minutes; jog for 10 minutes; walk for 5 minutes.
Wednesday:	Jog for 140 counts of your right foot, then walk for 20 counts of your right foot. Repeat the process for 20 minutes.
Thursday:	Walk for 3 minutes; jog at an easy pace for 14 minutes; walk for 3 minutes.
Friday:	Jog for 150 counts of your right foot, then walk for 20 counts of your right foot. Repeat the process for 20 minutes.
Saturday:	Jog for 20 minutes at an easy pace.

Week 10

Monday:	Jog at a comfortable, easy pace for 20 minutes.
Tuesday:	Jog at a fairly hard pace for 150 counts of your right foot, then jog at a very easy pace

(continued)	for 50 counts of your right foot. Repeat the process for 20 minutes.
Wednesday:	Jog at an easy pace for 20 minutes.
Thursday:	Run 10 intervals of 50 counts of your right foot at a medium pace, with a recovery interval of 50 counts of your right foot at a very easy jogging pace between each hard interval. Complete the 20 minutes with easy jogging.
Friday:	Jog at a comfortable, easy pace for 20 minutes.
Saturday:	Run from 12 to 15 intervals of 150 counts of your right foot, with a recovery interval of 50 counts of your right foot. Follow the interval session with 20 minutes of easy jogging.

Increase Your Training Mileage

The first step in becoming a racer is becoming a jogger, as we have just described. The next step is to increase your training mileage. In the jogging program, you probably ran between 12 and 21 miles each week. The more serious runners will want to run more mileage, so this section shows workouts that represent 10-mile increases in mileage from 20 miles to 80 miles a week. They are not a suggestion that you either want to or need to increase your mileage to that level.

If you want to run in road or track races, keep several points in mind. Running more mileage increases your chances of fast performances, but it does not guarantee them. Further, you can run many road races at a comfortable pace with the lowest level of training given here. As long as you set reasonable goals within the limits of your talent and training level, racing can be very enjoyable.

If you do increase your mileage, you should consider a hard/easy pattern of training weeks. Follow a harder, higher-mileage week with an easier, lower-mileage week. You should not go up to higher mileage until you have trained at a level below it for at least four weeks. The longer you train at any level, the easier it will be to move up to and train at the next higher level.

The easier weeks allow you to monitor your body more closely to learn how it is reacting to training. If training is always hard, fatigue may mask the early signs of injury or illness.

The acceleration runs mentioned here are a form of fartlek training. During this run, gradually accelerate to a speed faster than you can maintain for the entire training run; hold the faster pace for about 100 yards before slowing to the regular running pace. The exact distance of the run is not important.

Find a target, such as a tree, telephone pole or street corner, to run toward. Ease back on your pace when you reach the target. Street runners on short city blocks (about 100 yards or so) can accelerate for a block, then run easily for one or more blocks before accelerating again. The fartlek runs should be more exhilarating than exhausting.

Laying a Base: Weekly Mileage Patterns

One difference between a jogger and a serious runner is that the runner follows a training plan and has a goal. A person who wants to improve his marks at some distance, whether it be 800 meters, 10 kilometers, or the marathon, will plan training sessions that lead to that goal.

In the early stages of training, all runners are joggers. Until you have achieved a reasonable level of fitness, any attempt at serious training is likely to result in injury or illness, rather than improvement. The human body improves its workload gradually, rather than in large jumps. For this reason, you began with 10 weeks of "pre-season" training at the beginning level. This training gives you the first level or foundation in building toward a goal.

The next phase of training (after laying a foundation) is the base period, which is familiar to all serious runners. Weekly mileage patterns in the base period allow you to choose a training program that matches your ability and physical condition. It is important that you not try to do too much; remember the principle of moderation. If you are still tired before training on a given day, you may be training too hard or too much.

A good way to train with the following mileage patterns is to move back and forth, rather than use the same one every week. For example, if you train at the 40-mile-per-week level, you might range from 30 to 50 miles per week, averaging 40 miles a week over a longer period. The longer or "hard" weeks would be followed by shorter or "easy" weeks, in keeping with the principles of training and recovery. This variety will keep your training interesting, and allow your body to recover from the more difficult sessions.

Generally, it is best not to increase your mileage more than 10 miles from one week to the next. Larger increases in mileage add greater stresses to the body than you may realize. If you are in good physical condition, you may not realize the harmful effects until several weeks later. A few days of rest or easy training can help you to recover from fatigue. The effects of fatigue can include stress fractures, which normally require months of recovery, so it's wise not to overdo it.

Our rule of thumb is "easy up, easy down": The more gradual your training-load increase, the longer you should be able to train at a given level and maintain that condition, if you have to take a few days off for injury or illness.

Buildup of Mileage

20-Mile Week

Monday:	2-mile fartlek run.
Tuesday:	4-mile run at a steady pace. As your condition improves, pick up the tempo of the run.
Wednesday:	3-mile run at an easy, comfortable pace.
Thursday:	2-mile fartlek run. Include 8 accelerations of about 200 yards each.
Friday:	2-mile easy jog.
Saturday:	5-mile run, with variable pacing. Alternate running one mile hard, then one easy, and so on. If a mile is too far for a hard effort, use intervals of time instead, such as 5 minutes hard, then 5 easy, and so on.
Sunday:	2-mile run at a comfortable pace.

30-Mile Week

Monday:	4-mile fartlek run. Include 8 accelerations of 60 seconds or about 300 yards.
Tuesday:	6-mile run at steady pace. As your condition improves, pick up the tempo of the run.

Wednesday:	3-mile run at a comfortable pace.
Thursday:	5-mile fartlek run. If hills are available, run up several for about 200 yards. No hills: do 12 accelerations of about 200 yards each.
Friday:	2 miles of easy running on grass or other soft surface.
Saturday:	6-mile run, with variable pacing. Alternate running one mile hard, then one easy, and so on, timing yourself if necessary.
Sunday:	4-mile run at a comfortable pace.

40-Mile Week

Monday:	5-mile fartlek run. Include 6 accelerations of 2 minutes or about 600 yards.
Tuesday:	8-mile run at a gradually faster pace. Start easy, making each mile a little faster than the last one.
Wednesday:	4-mile run at a comfortable pace.
Thursday:	7-mile fartlek run. Include 12-20 accelerations of about 200 yards each or 35-40 seconds each.
Friday:	3 miles of easy running on grass or other soft surface.
Saturday:	8-mile run, with variable pacing. Alternate running two miles hard, then two easy, and so on, timing yourself if necessary.
Sunday:	5-mile comfortable run.

50-Mile Week

Monday:	7-mile fartlek run. Include 6 accelerations of 3 minutes of about 1000 yards.
Tuesday:	10-mile run at increasing pace. Start easy, making each 2-mile segment a little faster than the last one.
Wednesday:	5-mile run at a comfortable pace.
Thursday:	9-mile fartlek run. Include 24 accelerations of about 200 yards each or 35-40 seconds each.
Friday:	4 miles of easy running on grass or other soft surface.
Saturday:	10-mile run, with variable pacing. Run miles 3, 6 and 9 at a hard pace, with the other parts

(continued)	at a comfortable pace (i.e., 2 miles easy, then one hard, repeated three times).
Sunday:	6-mile easy run.

60-Mile Week

Monday:	8-mile fartlek run. Include 8 accelerations of 3 minutes or about 1000 yards.
Tuesday:	12-mile run at a steady, comfortable pace.
Wednesday:	6-mile very easy run.
Thursday:	10-mile fartlek run. Include 24 accelerations of about 200 yards or 35 seconds each.
Friday:	5 miles of very easy jogging on grass or other soft surface.
Saturday:	12-mile run, with variable pacing. Run a pattern of one mile easy, one mile at a medium pace, then one mile at a hard pace; repeat four times.
Sunday:	7 miles at a comfortable pace.

70-Mile Week

Monday:	9-mile fartlek run. Include 8 accelerations of 3 minutes or about 1000 yards.
Tuesday:	AM: 2-mile easy jog. PM: 12-mile run at a steady, comfortable pace.
Wednesday:	7-mile easy run.
Thursday:	AM: 2-mile easy run. PM: 10-mile fartlek run. Include 16 accelerations of about 200 yards.
Friday:	6 miles of easy running on grass or other soft surface.
Saturday:	AM: 12-mile run, following a pattern of one mile hard, then one mile easy, repeating for 12 miles. PM: 2-mile easy jog.
Sunday:	8 miles at a comfortable pace.

80-Mile Week

Monday:	10-mile fartlek run.
Tuesday:	AM: 4-mile easy run.

(continued)	PM: 12-mile run at a steady, comfortable pace.
Wednesday:	8-mile easy run.
Thursday:	AM: 4-mile easy run.
	PM: 10-mile fartlek run. Include 16-24 accelerations of about 200 yards.
Friday:	6 miles of easy jogging on grass or other soft surface.
Saturday:	AM: 10-mile steady run.
	PM: 5-mile run at relaxed pace.
Sunday:	10-mile easy run.

8. Training Schedules for the New Runner

Starting Training for
the 1500 Meters or One-Mile Run

The following program is for the runner who has been running regularly and has finished the 10-week beginner's program. You also must understand the basic training terms discussed in the book and have taken a Date Pace test and set a Goal Pace. You will be presented with a 21-day pre-season training pattern, a 14-day competitive pattern and a 10-day major competition pattern, similar to the training schedules of runners at Oregon.

Remember to warm up before your interval training sessions. It should include 10 to 15 minutes of easy jogging, some easy stretching exercises and two or three strides or medium-acceleration runs of about 100 meters each, with each one a bit faster than the one before it.

For the track sessions, remember that most outdoor tracks are 400 meters, though there are still many 440-yard tracks in the United States. An interval of 100 meters or 110 yards is one-fourth of a lap. The difference between 400 meters and 440 yards is only about 2½ yards, half a second or less for most runners. Because most tracks and race distances in the United States are being converted to 400 meters, most of the training schedules give the intervals in meters, though long runs are given in both miles and kilometers.

21-DAY PRE-SEASON PATTERN

Mon 1 30-40 minutes of varied fartlek. Include 8-12 spurts or accelerations of about 200 meters.

Tues 2 4-6 × 800 meters at Date Pace. Take a very easy 400-meter jog between each fast 800.
20 minutes of easy running.

Wed 3 30-40 minutes of steady running at a comfortable pace.

Thurs 4 16 × 100 meters at Goal Pace for the 1500 or mile. Jog 200 meters between each fast 100.
20 minutes of easy running.

Fri 5 20-40 minutes of easy running.

Sat 6 7-10 mile [12-16 km.] run.
Start at an easy pace and gradually increase the tempo, finishing at a hard pace you could not hold for the entire distance.

Sun 7 20-40 minutes easy running.

Mon 8 30-40 minutes of varied fartlek running. Include 20 × 100-meter (approx.) bursts at nearly full speed during the run.

Tues 9 5-7 miles [8-12 km.] run at a hard pace. If possible, do this over a measured course and time yourself.

Wed 10 Easy run for 20-40 minutes, depending on how you feel.

Thurs 11 10 × 150 meters at 1500 meters or mile Goal Pace. Take a 200-meter recovery interval between each fast 150.

Fri 12 Easy run, with the length depending upon how you feel.

Sat 13 4 × 1200 meters at 75 percent of Date Pace (see Table 4 for pace). Jog an easy 800 meters between each fast interval.
Easy jogging.

Sun 14 7-10 miles [12-16 km.] of very easy running.

Mon 15 30-40 minutes of varied fartlek running. Include 8-12 bursts of about 200 meters during the run.

Tues 16 6 × 300 meters at Goal Pace for 1500 meters or

mile. Jog an easy 300-meter recovery between each. 5-mile [8 km.] run at a comfortable pace.

Wed 17 20-40 minutes of easy running, with the time depending upon how you feel.

Thurs 18 3 × 600 meters at Goal Pace for 1500 meters or mile. Jog an easy 800-meter recovery interval after each 600.

5 × 200 meters at Date Pace for 1500 meters or mile. Jog an easy 200 meters between each fast 200.

20-minute easy run.

Fri 19 20-40 minutes of easy running.

Sat 20 1500-meter or one-mile Test Effort at 75 percent effort Date Pace. Accelerate the last 400 meters to full Date Pace. Record test effort results on progress chart.

5-mile [8 km.] easy run.

Sun 21 7-10 miles [12-16 km.] of very easy running.

14-DAY COMPETITIVE PATTERN

Mon 1 30-40 minutes varied fartlek run.

6 × 200 meters at Goal Pace for 1500 meters or mile. 30-second rest intervals.

Tues 2 3 × 800 meters at Goal Pace with 600-meter recovery jogs.

2 × 1500 meters or one mile at 75 percent effort Date Pace. Jog 800 meters between fast runs.

Easy run on the grass or other soft surface for 15 minutes.

Wed 3 30-40 minutes of running at a comfortable pace.

Thurs 4 6 × 300 meters at Goal Pace for 1500 meters or mile. 200-meter recovery jogs between each 300.

20-minute steady run at a comfortable pace.

4 × 100 meters at Goal Pace for 800 meters. Jog 100 meters between each fast 100.

Fri   **5**   20-30 minutes of easy running on the grass or other soft surface.

Sat   **6**   Competition. If possible, run a race shorter than your primary racing distance. If you normally run the 1500 or mile, run the 800 meters.

Sun   **7**   7-10 miles [12-16 km.] at an easy, comfortable pace.

Mon   **8**   4 × 200 meters at Goal Pace for 1500 meters or mile. Take 30-second rests for recovery interval. 30-minute steady run at a comfortable pace. 4 × 200 meters at Goal Pace for 1500 meters or mile. Take 30-second rests for recovery interval.

Tues   **9**   Run one set of 400-600-400-200 meters at Goal Pace for 1500 meters or mile, with a 300-meter recovery jog between fast intervals. This means to run:

1 × 400 meters at Goal Pace, 300-meter recovery jog;

1 × 600 meters at Goal Pace, 300-meter recovery jog;

1 × 400 meters at Goal Pace, 300-meter recovery jog;

1 × 200 meters at Goal Pace, 300-meter recovery jog.

3 × 800 meters at 75 percent effort Date Pace for 1500 or mile. Take a 400-meter recovery jog between fast intervals.

10 minutes of easy jogging on the grass or other soft surface.

Wed   **10**   30 minutes of easy running.

Thurs   **11**   3 × 400 meters at one to two seconds under your Goal Pace for the 1500 meters or mile run, with a 400-meter jog between each fast 400.

20 minutes of easy running on grass or other soft surface.

Fri   **12**   20 minutes of easy running on grass or other soft surface.

Sat   **13**   Competition. If possible, compete at the 1500 meters or one mile, or try to run 3000 meters or 2 miles.

Sun   **14**   7-10 miles [12-16 km] easy run.

10-DAY CHAMPIONSHIP PATTERN

Thurs **1**   Run 2½ laps [1000 meters] at Goal Pace for 1500 meters or mile. Take an easy 600-meter jog for recovery. Run 1½ laps [600 meters] at Goal Pace for 1500 meters or mile.
20-minute run on grass or other soft surface.

Fri   **2**   30-minute run at an easy pace on grass or other soft surface.

Sat   **3**   Run 3200 meters or 2 miles on the track at 50 percent of your Date Pace for the 1500 or mile.
30-minute run at a comfortable pace.

Sun   **4**   10-mile [16 km.] run at a comfortable pace.

Mon   **5**   40-minute varied fartlek run.

Tues **6**   Run 800 meters at full effort.
20-minute run on grass or other soft surface.
3 × 300 meters at Goal Pace for 1500 meters or mile. Take 200-meter jogs between each fast 300.

Wed   **7**   30-40 minutes running at a comfortable pace on grass or some other soft surface.

Thurs **8**   3 × 400 meters at Goal Pace for 1500 meters or mile. Take 200-meter recovery jogs between each fast 400. 20-minute run on grass or other soft surface.

Fri   **9**   30 minutes of easy running on grass or other soft surface.

Sat **10**   Competition.

Starting Training for
the 5000- and 10,000-Meter Runs

21-DAY PRE-SEASON PATTERN

Mon   **1**   40-60 minutes of varied-pace running.

Tues **2**   3 × 400 meters at Goal Pace, with 200-meter recovery jogs.

(continued) 2×1200 meters at Date Pace, with 600-meter recovery jogs.

10 minutes of easy running on grass or other soft surface.

Wed 3 30-40 minutes of easy running.

Thurs 4 40 minutes of varied pace running. Include 8-12 accelerated runs of about 300 meters.

Fri 5 20-40 minutes of easy running.

Sat 6 10-mile [16 km.] run over a measured course. Run at 50 percent effort of your 10,000 meters Date Pace (see Table 4).

Sun 7 8-12 mile [13-20 km.] run at a comfortable pace.

Mon 8 40-60 minutes of varied pace running. Include 16-24 accelerations of about 100 meters with 2 minutes of easy running between each acceleration.

Tues 9 4×400 meters at Goal Pace for 1500 meters or mile, with 400-meter recovery jogs (This Goal Pace is used for speedwork). 30 minutes of easy running.

Wed 10 30-40 minutes of easy running at a steady pace.

Thurs 11 3200 meters or 2 miles on the track (8 laps) at 75 percent effort Date Pace for the 10,000 meters.

5×300-meter cut-downs, with 300-meter recovery jogs. Run the first fast 300 at your Date Pace for 10,000 meters, then run each of the other 300s a bit faster than the one before it, running the last fast 300 at your Goal Pace for 1500 meters or one mile.

Fri 12 20-40 minutes of easy jogging.

Sat 13 4-6×mile or 1600 meters (4 laps) at 75 percent effort Date Pace for 5000 meters, with 800-meter recovery jogs. 10-15 minutes of easy jogging.

Sun 14 7-12 mile [12-20 km.] run at a comfortable pace.

Mon 15 40-60 minutes of varied pace running. Include several accelerations of different lengths, depending upon how you feel.

Tues 16 5×1000 meters (2½ laps) at Date Pace for 5000 meters, with 400-meter jogs between each fast interval.

10 minutes of easy jogging.

Wed 17 30-40 minutes of running at a steady, comfortable pace.

Thurs 18 Run one set of 400-600 400-200 meters at Goal Pace for 1500 meters or mile, with a 400-meter re-covery jog between fast intervals. This means to run:
1×400 meters at Goal Pace, 400 recovery jog.
1×600 meters at Goal Pace, 400 recovery jog.
1×400 meters at Goal Pace, 400 recovery jog.
1×200 meters at Goal Pace, 400 recovery jog.
20 minutes of easy running.

Fri 19 20-40 minutes of easy running.

Sat 20 Test effort for 5000 meters. If conditions are good, attempt to run at 75 percent effort Date Pace. 20-minute easy run.

Sun 21 40-minute easy run.

14-DAY COMPETITIVE PATTERN

Mon 1 40-minute varied fartlek run.
8×200 meters at Goal Pace for 1500 meters or mile, with 30-45 second recovery jogs.

Tues 2 6×800 meters at Goal Pace for 5000 meters. Take a 400-600-meter recovery jog between each fast 800.
20-minute easy run on grass or other soft surface.

Wed 3 40-minute steady run at a comfortable run.

Thurs 4 5×300 meters at Goal Pace for 1500 meters or mile, with 200-meter recovery jogs between each fast 300. 30-minute run at an easy pace on grass or other soft surface.

Fri 5 20-40 minutes of running on grass or other soft surface.

Sat 6 Competition. If possible, try to run an event either longer or shorter than your primary event. If your primary event is 5000 meters, try to run either the 1500/mile or the 10,000 meters.

Sun 7 40-minute run at an easy pace.

Mon 8 40-minute varied fartlek run.

(continued) 8-12 × 200 meters at Goal Pace for 1500 meters or mile, with 30-second recovery jogs.

Tues 9 Run 2½ laps, then 1½ laps at 1500 or mile pace, like this: Run 2½ laps [1 km.] at Goal Pace for 1500 meters or mile. Jog 800 meters (2 laps) for recovery; run 1½ laps (600 meters) at Goal Pace for 1500 meters or mile. After a rest, run 8 laps (2 miles or 3200 meters) at 75 percent effort Date Pace for 5000 meters. 10-20 minutes of easy running on grass or other soft surface.

Wed 10 30-40 minute run at a steady, comfortable pace.

Thurs 11 3 × 400 meters at Goal Pace for 1500 meters or mile, with 300-meter recovery jogs between each fast 400.

20-minute run on grass or other soft surface.

3 × 300 meters at Goal Pace for 5000 meters, with 100-meter recovery jogs between each fast 300.

Fri 12 20-40 minutes of easy running on grass or other soft surface.

Sat 13 Competition at 5000 meters.

Sun 14 8-12 miles [13-20 km.] at an easy pace.

10-DAY CHAMPIONSHIP PATTERN

Thurs 1 4 × 1200 meters (3 laps) at Goal Pace for 5000 meters. Take an 800-meter recovery jog after each fast 1200.

3 × mile or 1600 meters (4 laps) at Date Pace for 10,000 meters. Take an 800-meter recovery jog after each fast mile/1600.

Fri 2 20-40 minutes of easy running.

Sat 3 8 mile [13 km.] at a medium pace.

Sun 4 Easy run of 8-12 miles [13-20 km.].

Mon 5 40-minute run at varied pace.

Tues 6 1 × 1200 meters (3 laps) at Goal Pace for 1500 meters or mile.

30-minute easy run.

(continued) 3 × 300 meters at Goal Pace for 5000 meters, with 200-meter recovery jog between each fast 300.

Wed 7 30-40 minute run at a steady, comfortable pace.

Thurs 8 4 miles or 6400 meters (16 laps) at 50 percent effort Date Pace for 5000 or 10,000 meters.

Fri 9 20-30 minutes easy running on grass or other soft surface.

Sat 10 Competition at 5000 or 10,000 meters.

9. Elite Training Schedules

TRAINING SCHEDULES BY EVENT

Cross-Country

These cross-country workouts are designed for national-level college-age male athletes who run or desire to run in the 29:00 to 30:00 range for 10,000 meters. You should keep this in mind as you design your own training based on this pattern. Running times should be scaled to your own level of ability and experience, rather than trying to do these exact workouts.

Because the Oregon cross-country season is brief (two to four races), there is more intensive interval training than you would do for a longer schedule with more races in the season.

Runners at Oregon are asked to begin their summers with 30- to 50-mile [50-80 km.] running weeks, building to 60 to 70 miles [95-115 km.] a week in September when school starts.

You should hold an interval workout on a grassy surface, such as a golf course, twice a week. Moderately hard runs of 10-12 miles [16-20 km.] are recommended twice a week. After the cross-country season, return to a fartlek-based training program.

21-DAY TRAINING PATTERN

Mon   **1**   *AM:* 4-7 miles [6-12 km.].
             PM: 60-minute fartlek run.
Tues **2**   *AM:* 4-7 miles [6-12 km.].

Cross-country. Consistency is the keyword for team success in cross-country. Alberto Salazar, Rudy Chapa and Don Clary stay together in a 1978 race in Eugene.

(continued)   *PM:* 4×1200 meters at your 10,000 meters Goal Pace (400-meter rest).

3×mile or 1600 meters in 5:00—4:48—4:32 (800-meter rest), like this:

1×1600 or mile in 5:00, jog 800 meters.

1×1600 or mile in 4:48, jog 800 meters.

1×1600 or mile in 4:32, jog 800 meters.

Easy run (20-30 min.) on grass or other soft surface.

Wed   **3**   *AM:* 4-7 miles [6-12 km.].

PM: 5-10 mile steady run [8-16 km.].

Thurs   **4**   *AM:* 4-7 miles [6-12 km.].

PM: 9×300 uphill (3× easy; 3× medium; 3× hard).

30-minute run.

Fri   **5**   *AM:* Easy run (20-30 min.).

PM: Easy run (20-30 min.).

Sat   **6**   *10:00 AM:* Simulation drill with 10-mile run [16 km.], run like this:

(1) Run 1200 on track in 3:15 (60-65-70 splits).

(2) Run 10 miles at 6-minute pace, with a 1200 or ¾ mile at a steady 67 pace included (3:21 total)

(3) Finish with a 1200 on the track, reversing the pacing of the starting 1200, i.e. 70, then 65, then 60 seconds on successive laps.

Sun   **7**   12-15 miles of easy running [20-25 km.].

Mon   **8**   *AM:* 4-7 miles [6-12 km.].

PM: 45-minute fartlek run.

Tues   **9**   *AM:* 4-7 miles [6-12 km.].

PM: 10-mile controlled run [16 km.], timing each mile; alternate 6:00 and 5:00 miles, i.e., first mile in 6 minutes, second mile in 5 minutes, third mile in 6 minutes, etc.

Wed   **10**   *AM:* 4-7 miles easy [6-12 km.].

PM: 4-7 miles easy [6-12 km.].

Thurs   **11**   *AM:* 4-7 miles [6-12 km.].

PM: 9×300 meters uphill (3× easy; 3× medium; 3× hard). Jog to starting point for recovery.

Easy run (20-30 min.).

Fri   **12**   *AM:* Easy run (20-30 min.).

PM: Easy run (20-30 min.).

Sat   **13**   *10:00 AM:* 6×1 mile cut-downs, with 400-meter rests. Start at 5:20, making each mile faster, finishing at about 4:32 for the last mile, like this:
1×mile in 5:20, jog 400 meters.
1×mile in 5:10, jog 400 meters.
1×mile in 5:00, jog 400 meters.
1×mile in 4:50, jog 400 meters.
1×mile in 4:40, jog 400 meters.
1×mile in 4:32, jog 400 meters.

Sun   **14**   12-15 miles of easy running [20-25 km.].

Mon   **15**   *AM:* 4-7 miles [6-12 km.].
PM: 40-minute fartlek run.

Tues   **16**   *AM:* 4-7 miles [6-12 km.].
PM: 3× (1200-800-400) on grass with 400-meter rests; run at 10,000 meters Goal Pace like this:
1×1200 meters, jog 400 meters.
1×800 meters, jog 400 meters.
1×400 meters, jog 400 meters.
Easy run (20-30 min.) on grass.

Wed   **17**   *AM:* 4-7 miles [6-12 km.].
PM: 4-7 miles [6-12 km.].

Thurs   **18**   *AM:* 4-7 miles [6-12 km.].
PM: 9×300 meters uphill (3× easy; 3× medium; 3× hard).
30-minute easy run.

Fri   **19**   *AM:* Easy run (20-30 min.).
PM: Easy run (20-30 min.).

Sat   **20**   *10:00 AM:* 10-mile simulation drill [16 km.].
(1) Start with 1200 on track, at 60-65-70 pace.
(2) 10 miles at 6:00 pace, with a middle 1200 at 3:12-3:18 64-66 seconds pace for 400 meters, steady surge.
(3) Finish with 1200 on track in 70 seconds, then 65 seconds and finally 60 seconds for the last 400.

Sun   **21**   12-15 miles of easy running [20-25 km.].

14-DAY COMPETITION PATTERN

Mon   **1**   *AM:* 4-7 miles [6-12 km.].
PM: 40-minute fartlek run.

Tues   **2**   *AM:* 4-mile controlled [tempo] run at 5:00 per mile.

          PM: 1 × mile at Goal Pace for 10,000 meters, jog 400 meters.

          2 × 1200 at Goal Pace for 5000 meters, jog 400 meters.

          3 × 800 at Date Pace for 1500 meters, jog 400 meters.

          4 × 400 cut-downs, jog 200 meters.

Wed   **3**   *AM:* 4-7 miles [6-12 km.].

          PM: 7-10 miles at a comfortable pace [11-16 km.].

Thurs **4**   *AM:* 4-7 miles [6-12 km.].

          PM: 9 × 300 uphill (3 × easy; 3 × medium, 3 × hard).

          30-minute run.

Fri   **5**   *AM:* Easy run (20-30 min.).

          PM: Easy run (20-30 min.).

Sat   **6**   *10:00 AM:* 1 × mile in 4:08-4:12. If no competition, run at 75 percent Goal Pace.

          10 miles at 6:20 pace.

          PM: Easy run (20-30 min.).

Sun   **7**   12-15 miles at a comfortable pace [20-25 km.].

Mon   **8**   *AM:* 5-mile control run at 5:20 per mile [8 km.].

          PM: 45-minute fartlek run.

Tues   **9**   *AM:* 4-7 miles [6-12 km.].

          PM: 1 × mile at 5000 meters Goal Pace.

          5-mile run at 6:20 pace [8 km.].

          1 × mile at 5000 meters Goal Pace.

Wed **10**   *AM:* 4-7 miles [6-12 km.].

          PM: 5-8 miles at steady pace [8-13 km.].

Thurs **11**   *AM:* 4-7 miles [6-12 km.].

          PM: 1 × 1200 at 5000 meters Goal Pace, jog 400 meters.

          5-mile easy run.

          3 × 300 cut-downs, jog 100 meters.

Fri   **12**   *AM:* Easy run (20-30 min.).

          PM: Easy run (20-30 min.).

Sat   **13**   *AM:* Cross-Country Race.

Sun   **14**   12-17 miles easy run [20-27 km.].

800-Meter Run Training

These workouts are designed for national- to international-level college-age male athletes who run or desire to run in the 1:45 to 1:48 range for 800 meters. You should keep this in mind as you design your own training based on this pattern. Any running times should be scaled to your own level of ability and experience, rather than trying to do these exact workouts. This set of schedules is designed for the 800-meter specialist who is more of a 400-meter runner than a 1500-meter runner. The 800 runner who leans toward the 1500 meters as his strength may prefer to use the schedules given under 1500-meter run training.

800 meters. The shortest of the middle-distance events requires the right combination of endurance and speed training. Don Paige wins the 1980 Olympic Trials on Hayward Field's wet track.

21-DAY PRE-SEASON PATTERN

Mon 1 (1) 1×600 meters cut-downs (600-500-400-300-200-100), run like this:

> 1×600, passing 400 in 75 seconds, 200-meter recovery jog.

(continued)   1 × 500, passing 400 in 70 seconds, jog 200 meters.

1 × 400 in 65 seconds, jog 200 meters.

1 × 300 in 47 seconds, jog 100 meters.

1 × 200 in 30 seconds, jog 100 meters.

1 × 100 in 13 seconds, jog 100 meters.

(2) 20-minute run on grass or other soft surface.

Tues   **2**   (1) 30-minute run.

(2) Weight program.

Wed   **3**   (1) 3 × 200 sets (800 rests between sets), run like this:

1 × 200 in 32 seconds, jog 200 meters.

1 × 200 in 32 seconds, jog 200 meters.

1 × 200 in 32 seconds, jog 800 meters.

This is the end of the first set. Run the second set in 30 seconds and the last set in 28 seconds. These times will speed up until during the season you might run the first set in 27 seconds, the next set in 25 seconds, and the last set in 22-23 seconds.

(2) 5 × 200 cut-downs (33-31-29-27-25) with 200-meter rests.

Thurs   **4**   (1) 30-minute run.

(2) Weight program.

Fri   **5**   (1) 5 × 300 at 800 meters Goal Pace, with 300-meter recovery jogs.

(2) 20-minute run.

Sat   **6**   (1) 30-minute run.

(2) Weight program.

Sun   **7**   (1) 5-mile run [8 km.].

Mon   **8**   (1) 5 × 500 up a gradual hill, jog back down the hill to recover.

(2) Easy run (20-30 min.).

Tues   **9**   (1) 8 × 100 in 12 seconds with 100-200 rests.

(2) Easy run (20-30 min.).

(3) Weight routine.

Wed   **10**   5-mile run at steady pace [8 km.].

Thurs   **11**   (1) Easy run (20-30 min.).

(2) Weights.

Fri   **12**   (1) 800 Simulation Drill #1: Run 800 meters like this:

First 100 meters at Goal Pace.

Middle 600 meters at 80 seconds pace for 400 meters.

Last 100 meters at Goal Pace.

(2) 4 × 150 meters: Accelerate 50 meters.

Float 50 meters.

Accelerate 50 meters. Recover with a jog-walk of 250-650 meters.

Sat   **13**   (1) 800 Simulation Drill #2: Run 800 meters like this:

First 100 meters at Goal Pace.

Next 200 meters in 40 seconds.

Next 100 meters (to the 400 mark) at Goal Pace.

Next 300 meters in 60 seconds.

Last 100 meters at Goal Pace.

(2) 5 × 300 cut-downs, with 100-meter jogs. Begin at Date Pace and end faster than Goal Pace.

Sun   **14**   5-mile comfortable run [8 km.].

Mon   **15**   (1) 1 × 600 set: 600 at 70 pace; 500 at 65 pace; 400 at 60 pace; 300 in 43 seconds; 200 in 26 seconds; 100 in 11.5 seconds (see Day 1).

(2) 3-mile run [5 km.].

Tues   **16**   (1) 30-minute run.

(2) Weight program.

Wed   **17**   (1) 12 × 100 in 12 seconds with 100- to 200-meter rests.

(2) Easy run (20-30 min.).

Thurs **18**   (1) 800 Simulation Drill #3: Run 800 meters like this:

First 200 meters at Goal Pace.

Middle 400 meters in 80 seconds.

Last 200 meters at Goal Pace.

(2) Easy run (20-30 min.).

(3) 5 × 300 cut-downs with 100-meter jogs, starting at Date Pace.

Fri   **19**   (1) 3 × 400 cut-downs (55-53-51) with 400-meter rests.

(2) Easy run (20-30 min.) on grass or other soft surface.

Sat   **20**   (1) 800-meter Test Effort at Date Pace

(2) 5-mile run [5 km.].

(3) 6 × 300 cut-downs (from Date Pace to Goal Pace), with 100-meter jogs.

(4) Easy weight training session.

Sun   **21**   5-mile run [8 km.].

14-DAY COMPETITIVE PATTERN

Mon   **1**   (1) 500-300-150 at Goal Pace, run like this:

1 × 500 meters at Goal Pace, jog 500 meters.

1 × 300 meters at Goal Pace, jog 300 meters.

1 × 150 meters at Goal Pace, jog 150 meters.

(2) 5 × 200 at Goal Pace, with 200-meter recovery jogs.

(3) Easy run (20-30 min.) on grass or other soft surface.

Tues   **2**   (1) 12 × 100 in 12 seconds with 100-meter rests.

(2) Easy run (20-30 min.) on grass.

(3) Easy weight training program.

Wed   **3**   (1) 1 × 600 at 800 meters Goal Pace, then a 600-meter jog.

(2) 5 × 300 cut-downs (from Date Pace to Goal Pace), taking 100-meter rests.

(3) Easy weight training program.

Thurs   **4**   (1) Easy run (20-30 min.) on grass.

(2) Easy weight work.

Fri   **5**   (1) 800 Simulation Drill #4: Run 800 meters like this:

First 300 meters at Goal Pace.

Next 300 meters in 60 seconds.

Last 200 meters at Goal Pace.

(2) Easy run (20-30 min.) on grass.

Sat   **6**   *Races:* (1) Open 400 meters, (2) 4 × 400 relay.

PM: Weight training routine.

Sun   7   5-mile run [8 km.].

Mon   8   (1) Long 600 set (times are with flying starts).

          1 × 600 at 65 seconds for 400, 200-meter rest.

          1 × 500 at 60 seconds for 400, 200-meter rest.

          1 × 400 in 55 seconds, 200-meter rest.

          1 × 300 in 40 seconds, 100-meter rest.

          1 × 200 in 25 seconds, 100-meter rest.

          1 × 100 in 11 seconds, 100-meter rest.

        (2) Easy run (20-30 min.) on grass.

Tues   9   (1) 3 × 150 meters sprint-float-sprint drill. Accelerate for 50 meters, float for 50 meters, then accelerate for 50 meters. Jog 250-650 meters to recover.

        (2) 3 × 150 meters float-sprint-float drill. Float for 50 meters, accelerate for 50 meters, then float for 50 meters. Jog 250-650 meters to recover.

        (3) Easy run (20-30 min.) on grass.

        (4) Weight training routine.

Wed   10   (1) 5 × 300 cut-downs, reaching the 200 in 28-26-25-24-23 seconds. Jog 100 meters after each.

        (2) Easy run (20-30 min.) on grass.

Thurs 11   (1) Easy run (20-30 min.) on grass.

        (2) Easy weight routine.

Fri   12   (1) Easy run (20-30 min.) on grass.

        (2) 2 × 100 meters in 12 seconds.

Sat   13   *Races:* (1) 800 meters; (2) 4 × 1600 relay, if possible.

        PM: Weight training routine.

Sun   14   (1) 800 Simulation Drill #5: Run 800 meters like this:

         First 300 meters at Goal Pace.

         Middle 200 meters in 45 seconds.

         Last 300 meters at Goal Pace.

        (2) Easy run (20-30 min.) on grass.

10-DAY CHAMPIONSHIP PATTERN

Thurs   1   (1) Long 600-meter set (times are with flying starts), run like this:

(continued) 1 × 600 at 57 seconds for 400 meters, jog 200 meters.

1 × 500 at 55 seconds for 400 meters, jog 200 meters.

1 × 400 in 53 seconds, jog 200 meters.

1 × 300 in 38 seconds, jog 100 meters.

1 × 200 in 24 seconds, jog 100 meters.

1 × 100 in 11 seconds, jog 100 meters.

(2) Easy run (20-30 min.) on grass.

Fri 2 *11:00 AM:* 4 × 100 meters in 11 seconds with 200-meter rests. Times are with a flying start. *PM:* Easy run (20-30 min.) on grass or other soft surface.

Sat 3 (1) 1 × 600 at 51-52 seconds for 400 meters, jog 600 meters.

(2) 5 × 200 in 24-26 seconds with 200-meter rests.

(3) Easy run (20-30 min.) on grass or other soft surface.

Sun 4 5 miles at a comfortable pace [8 km.].

Mon 5 *11:00 AM:* 3 × 150 meters float-sprint-float drill. *PM:* 30-minute run on grass or other soft surface.

Tues 6 (1) 5 × 200 in 25 seconds with 200-meter rests.

(2) Easy run (20-30 min.) on grass or other soft surface.

Wed 7 Easy run (20-30 min.) on grass or other soft surface. Include 2-4 × 135 meters striding.

Thurs 8 800 meters Qualifying Heats.

Fri 9 800 meters Semifinals.

Sat 10 800 meters Finals.

The 800-Meter Simulation Drills
(Used in the 800 and 1500 training pattern):

800 Simulation Drill #1: Run 800 meters like this:
First 100 meters at Goal Pace.
Middle 600 at 80 seconds pace for 400 meters.
Last 100 at Goal Pace.

800 Simulation Drill #2: Run 800 meters like this:
First 100 at Goal Pace.
Next 200 in 40 seconds.

1500 meters. Training for the metric mile encompasses quality pace-work, speedwork and long runs. Mary Decker had little trouble winning the 1980 Olympic Trials for 1500 meters.

(continued)   Next 100 (to the 400 mark) at Goal Pace.
Next 300 in 60 seconds.
Last 100 at Goal Pace.

800 Simulation Drill #3: Run 800 meters like this:
First 200 at Goal Pace.
Middle 400 in 80 seconds.
Last 200 at Goal Pace.

800 Simulation Drill #4: Run 800 meters like this:
First 300 meters at Goal Pace.
Next 300 in 60 seconds.
Last 200 at Goal Pace.

800 Simulation Drill #5: Run 800 meters like this:
First 300 at Goal Pace.
Middle 200 in 45 seconds.
Last 300 at Goal Pace.

800 Simulation Drill #6: Run 800 meters like this:
First 400 at Goal Pace.
Next 200 in 45 seconds.
Last 200 at Goal Pace.

800 Simulation Drill #7: Run 800 meters like this:
First 200 at Goal Pace.
Next 200 in 45 seconds.
Last 400 at Goal Pace.

800 Simulation Drill #8: Run 800 meters like this:
First 500 at Goal Pace.
Next 200 in 45 seconds.
Last 100 at Goal Pace.

800 Simulation Drill #9: Run 800 meters like this:
First 100 at Goal Pace.
Next 200 in 45 seconds.
Last 500 at Goal Pace.

1500- and 800-Meter Run Training

These workouts are designed for national- to international-level college-age male athletes who run or desire to run in the 3:35 to 3:39 range for 1500 meters or 1:45 to 1:48 for 800 meters. You should keep this in mind as you design your own training based on this pattern. Any running times should be scaled to your own level of ability and experience, rather than trying to do these exact workouts.

21-DAY PRE-SEASON PATTERN

Mon 1 *AM:* 3-5 miles easy [5-8 km.].
  PM: (1) 40-minute fartlek run.
  (2) Weight training routine.

Tues 2 *AM:* 3-5 miles easy [5-8 km.].
  PM: Control (tempo) run: 8 miles [13 km.] at 5:30-6:00 per mile. Check the time each mile.

Wed 3 *AM:* 3-5 miles easy.
  PM: (1) 30-40 minutes run at steady pace.
  (2) Weight training routine.

Thurs 4 *AM:* 3-5 miles easy.
  PM: (1) 3 × 400 quick (begin with 60 seconds), with 400-meter rests. Cut time gradually to 52 seconds before season begins.
  (2) 30-minute run.
  (3) 3 × 300 meter cut-downs, 100-meter jogs.

Fri 5 *AM:* Easy run (20-30 min.).
  PM: (1) Easy run (20-30 min.).
  (2) Weight training routine.

Sat 6 *AM:* Easy run (20-30 min.).
  PM: (1) 800-meter Simulation Drill. Begin with Drill #1 and work to Drill #9 by start of season.
  (2) 5-mile run [8 km.].
  (3) 9 × 300 cut-downs, 100-meter rests.

Sun 7 8-12 mile steady run [13-20 km.].

Mon 8 *AM:* 3-5 miles easy [5-8 km.].
  PM: (1) 40-minute fartlek run.
  (2) Weight training routine.

Tues 9 *AM:* 3-5 miles easy [5-8 km.].
  PM: (1) Intervals at Goal Pace for the 1500 meters or mile, run like this:
  1 × 400 at Goal Pace, 200-meter rest.
  1 × 600 at Goal Pace, 200-meter rest.
  1 × 400 at Goal Pace, 200-meter rest.
  1 × 200 at Goal Pace, 200-meter rest.

(continued) (2) 7-mile run at 5:30 per mile [11 km.].

Wed 10 *AM:* 3-5 miles easy [5-8 km.].

PM: (1) 7-10 miles [11-16 km.] at a comfortable pace.

(2) Weight training routine.

Thurs 11 *AM:* 3-5 miles easy [5-8 km.].

PM: 5-mile control (tempo) run [8 km.]; begin at 6:00 per mile and try to reach 5:00 per mile by the start of the season.

Fri 12 *AM:* Easy run (20-30 min.).

PM: (1) Easy run (20-30 min.).

(2) Weight training routine.

Sat 13 *AM:* Easy run (20-30 min.).

PM: (1) Intervals on soft surface, if possible. 6 × 800 with 200-meter rests. Begin at 2:30 at first, dropping to 2:12 by the start of the racing season. 6 × 300 cut-downs around 50 seconds, with 100-meter rests.

(2) Easy run (20-30 min.).

Sun 14 8-12 mile easy run [13-20 km.].

Mon 15 *AM:* 3-5 miles easy [5-8 km.].

PM: (1) 40-minute fartlek run.

(2) Weight training routine.

Tues 16 *AM:* 3-5 miles easy [5-8 km.].

PM: (1) 8-mile control (tempo) run [13 km.].

(2) 6 × 300 cut-downs, with 100-meter rests. Begin with a comfortable pace, increasing the speed of each fast 300 until the last one is at 90 percent effort.

Wed 17 *AM:* 3-5 miles easy [5-8 km.].

PM: (1) 30-minute easy run.

(2) Weight training routine.

Thurs 18 *AM:* 3-5 miles easy [5-8 km.].

PM: (1) 3 × 400 quick, with 400-meter recoveries. Begin at 60 seconds, gradually dropping to 52 seconds by the start of the season.

(2) 20-minute run on grass or other soft surface.

(3) 3 × 300 cut-downs with 100-meter rests.

Fri **19** *AM:* Easy run (20-30 min.) on grass or other soft surface.

PM: (1) Easy run (20-30 min.) on grass or other soft surface.

(2) Weight training routine.

Sat **20** *AM:* Easy run (20-30 min.).

PM: (1) 1500-meter or one-mile trial at Date Pace.

(2) 5-mile run [8 km.].

(3) 9 × 300 cut-downs, with 100-meter rests.

Sun **21** 8-12 miles at a comfortable pace [13-20 km.].

14-DAY COMPETITIVE PATTERN

Mon **1** *AM:* 3-5 miles easy [5-8 km.].

PM: 45-minute fartlek run.

Tues **2** *AM:* 3-5 miles easy [5-8 km.].

PM: (1) Intervals at Goal Pace for 1500 meters or mile.

1 × 400 at Goal Pace, jog 200 meters.

1 × 600 at Goal Pace, jog 200 meters.

1 × 400 at Goal Pace, jog 200 meters.

1 × 200 at Goal Pace, jog 200 meters.

(2) 4 × 800-300 drill on sawdust. Run 800 meters at Date Pace, jog 200 meters, then run 300 meters at Goal Pace, jog 300 meters. Repeat 4 times, running the fast intervals faster (like cut-downs) each time.

PM: (3) Easy run (20-30 min.).

Wed **3** *AM:* 3-5 miles easy [5-8 km.].

PM: (1) 30-40 min. run on grass or other soft surface.

(2) Weight training routine.

Thurs **4** *AM:* 3-5 miles easy [5-8 km.].

PM: (1) 3 × 150 meters sprint-float-sprint drill.

Accelerate for 50 meters.

Float for 50 meters.

Accelerate for 50 meters.

(continued)   (2) 20-minute run on grass or other soft surface.

Fri   5   *AM:* 3-5 miles easy [5-8 km.].
           PM: 800 Simulation Drill; begin with Drill #1, progressing to Drill #5 by the end of the racing season.

Sat   6   *AM:* 800-meter race.
           PM: Weight training routine.

Sun   7   (1) 800 Simulation Drill; begin with Drill #5, progressing to Drill #9 by the end of the racing season.
           (2) Easy run (20-30 min.) on grass or other soft surface.

Mon   8   *AM:* 3-5 miles easy [5-8 km.].
           PM: (1) 40-minute fartlek run.
           (2) Weight training routine.

Tues   9   *AM:* 3-6 miles easy [5-10 km.].
           PM: (1) 3 × 800 at 1500 meters or mile Goal Pace with 400-meter rests.
           (2) 6 × 300 cut-downs, with 100-meter jogs.

Wed   10   *AM:* 4-7 miles easy [6-11 km.].
           PM: (1) 4-7 miles at a steady pace [6-11 km.].
           (2) Weight training routine.

Thurs 11   *AM:* 3-5 miles easy [5-8 km.].
           PM: (1) 3 × 400 in 53-55 seconds, with 400-meter jogs.
           (2) Easy run (20-30 min.) on grass or other soft surface.

Fri   12   *AM:* Easy run (20-30 min.) on grass or other soft surface.
           PM: Easy run (20-30 min.) on grass or other soft surface.

Sat   13   *AM:* 1500-meter or one-mile race.
           PM: Weight training routine.

Sun   14   8-12 miles [13-20 km.].

10-DAY CHAMPIONSHIP PATTERN

Thurs 1   *AM:* Easy run (20-30 min.).
           PM: (1) 800-meter time trial at full effort.

(continued)   (2) 30-minute run on grass or other soft surface.

Fri   **2**   *AM:* 20-minute run on grass or other soft surface.

11:00 AM: 2 × 200 in 24 seconds, with 200-meter jog.

PM: Easy run (20-30 min.) on grass or other soft surface.

Sat   **3**   *AM:* Easy run (20-30 min.) on grass or other soft surface.

PM: (1) Intervals at 1500 meters or mile Goal Pace.

1 × 1000 meters, jog 600 meters.

1 × 600 meters, jog 600 meters.

(2) 5 × 300 cut-downs, with 100-meter jogs.

(3) Easy run (20-30 min.) on grass or other soft surface.

Sun   **4**   7-9 mile run [11-15 km.].

Mon   **5**   *AM:* 3-5 miles easy [5-8 km.].

11:00 AM: 3 × 300 in 40.5 seconds with 200-meter rests.

PM: 20-30 min. run on grass or other soft surface.

Tues   **6**   *AM:* 3-5 miles easy [5-8 km.].

PM: (1) 3 × 400 in 54-56 seconds with 400-meter rests.

(2) Easy run (20-30 min.) on grass or other soft surface.

Wed   **7**   *AM:* Easy run (20-30 min.) on grass or other soft surface.

PM: Easy run (20-30 min.) on grass or other soft surface.

Thurs   **8**   Trial Heats: 800 meters or 1500 meters.

Fri   **9**   Semifinals, if necessary. If no race, easy run (20-30 min.) on grass or other soft surface.

Sat   **10**   Finals in 800-meter or 1500-meter run.

The 1500-Meter Simulation Drills
(Used in the 1500 and 5000 training patterns):

1500 Simulation Drill #1: Run 1600 meters or mile like this:
First 200 meters at Goal Pace.
Next 3 laps at 75-80 seconds for 400 meters.

Last 200 at Goal Pace.

1500 Simulation Drill #2: Run 1600 meters or mile like this:
First 200 at Goal Pace.
Next 500 at 75-80 seconds for 400 meters.
Middle 200 at Goal Pace.
Next 500 at 75-80 seconds for 400 meters.
Last 200 at Goal Pace.

1500 Simulation Drill #3: Run 1600 meters or mile like this:
First 300 at Goal Pace.
Next 2½ laps at 75-80 seconds for 400 meters.
Last 300 at Goal Pace.

1500 Simulation Drill #4: Run 1600 meters or mile like this:
First 300 at Goal Pace.
Next 400 in 75-80 seconds.
Middle 200 at Goal Pace.
Next 400 in 75-80 seconds.
Last 300 at Goal Pace.

1500 Simulation Drill #5: Run 1600 meters or mile like this:
First 400 at Goal Pace.
Middle 800 at 75-80 seconds for 400 meters.
Last 400 at Goal Pace.

1500 Simulation Drill #6: Run 1600 meters or mile like this:
First 400 at Goal Pace.
Next 300 in 60 seconds (80 seconds for 400).
Middle 200 at Goal Pace.
Next 300 in 60 seconds.
Last 400 at Goal Pace.

1500 Simulation Drill #7: Run 1600 meters or mile like this:
First 500 at Goal Pace.
Middle 600 at 80 seconds for 400 meters.
Last 500 at Goal Pace.

1500 Simulation Drill #8: Run 1600 meters or mile like this:
First 500 at Goal Pace.
Next 200 in 45 seconds.
Middle 200 at Goal Pace.
Next 200 in 45 seconds.
Last 500 at Goal Pace.

1500 Simulation Drill #9: Run 1600 meters or mile like this:
First 600 at Goal Pace.

Middle 400 in 80-90 seconds.

Last 600 at Goal Pace.

1500 Simulation Drill #10: Run 1600 meters or mile like this:

First 800 at Goal Pace.

Next 400 in 80-90 seconds.

Last 400 at Goal Pace.

1500 Simulation Drill #11: Run 1600 meters or mile like this:

First 900 at Goal Pace.

Next 400 in 80-90 seconds.

Last 300 at Goal Pace.

1500 Simulation Drill #12: Run 1600 meters or mile like this:

First 2½ laps at Goal Pace.

Next 400 in 90 seconds.

Last 200 at Goal Pace.

1500 Simulation Drill #13: Run 1600 meters or mile like this:

First 2½ laps at Goal Pace.

Next 300 in 60-70 seconds (80-90 seconds for 400).

Last 300 at Goal Pace.

1500- and 5000-Meter Run Training

These workouts are designed for national- to international-level college-age male athletes who run or desire to run 3:35 to 3:39 for 1500 meters or under 13:45 for 5000 meters. You should keep this in mind as you design your own training based on this pattern. Any running times should be scaled to your own level of ability and experience, rather than trying to do these exact workouts and leaving your best race on the track.

21-DAY PRE-SEASON PATTERN

Mon   **1**   *AM:* 4-6 miles easy [6-10 km.].

PM: (1) 45-minute fartlek run.

(2) 8×200 in 30 seconds with 30-second recoveries.

Tues   **2**   *AM:* 4-6 miles easy [6-10 km.].

PM: 6×800-meter/300-meter drill on sawdust or grass trail. Each 800-meter is faster than the

5000 meters. So fast has this "distance" race become, many milers train to incorporate the 5000 meters. Alberto Salazar leads in a heat of the 5000 meters at the 1980 Olympic Trials. Centrowitz won the finals.

(continued)   last one (cut-downs), while each 300 is 50 seconds.

Run them like this:

1 × 800, jog 200 meters, run 300 in 50 seconds, jog 300 meters.

1 × 800 a bit faster, jog 200, run 300 in 50 seconds, jog 300.

1 × 800 a bit faster, jog 200, run 300 in 50 seconds, jog 300.

1 × 800 a bit faster, jog 200, run 300 in 50 seconds, jog 300.

1 × 800 a bit faster, jog 200, run 300 in 50 seconds, jog 300.

1 × 800 a bit faster, jog 200, run 300 in 50 seconds, jog 300.

Wed   **3**   *AM:* 4-6 miles easy [6-10 km.].

            PM: 45-minute steady run at 6:20 per mile.

Thurs   **4**   *AM:* 4-6 miles easy [6-10 km.].

(continued) *PM:* (1) 3 × 400 quick [begin with 60 seconds] with 400-meter rests. Cut the time gradually to 53 seconds by end of racing season.

(2) 30-minute run.

Fri 5 *AM:* Easy run (20-30 min.).

PM: Easy run (20-30 min.).

Sat 6 *AM:* Easy run (20-30 min.).

PM: 10-mile control (tempo) run at 5:12-5:20 per mile [16 km.].

Sun 7 12-15 miles at a comfortable pace [20-25 km.].

Mon 8 *AM:* 4-6 miles easy [6-10 km.].

PM: (1) 45-minute fartlek run.

(2) 6 × 200 in 30 seconds with 30-second recoveries.

Tues 9 *AM:* 4-6 miles easy [6-10 km.].

PM: 10-mile control (tempo) run at 5:30-5:40 per mile [16 km.].

Wed 10 *AM:* 4-6 miles easy [6-10 km.].

PM: 45-minute steady run at a comfortable pace.

Thurs 11 *AM:* 4-6 miles easy [6-10 km.].

PM: (1) Intervals at Goal Pace for 1500 meters or mile.

1 × 400 at Goal Pace, jog 200 meters.

1 × 600 at Goal Pace, jog 200 meters.

1 × 400 at Goal Pace, jog 200 meters.

1 × 200 at Goal Pace, jog 200 meters.

(2) 30-minute run at a comfortable pace.

Fri 12 *AM:* 20-minute easy run.

PM: 20-30 min. easy run.

Sat 13 *AM:* Easy run (20-30 min.).

PM: (1) 5000 meters Simulation Drill #1: Run 1600 meters or mile like this:

First 200 at Goal Pace.

Next 3 laps at 75-80 seconds per 400 meters.

Last 200 at Goal Pace.

(2) 7-mile run at a comfortable pace [11 km.].

Sun 14 12-15 miles at a comfortable pace [20-25 km.].

Mon 15 *AM:* 4-6 miles easy [6-10 km.].

(continued) *PM:* (1) 45-minute fartlek run.

(2) 10×200 in 30 seconds with 30-second recoveries.

Tues 16 *AM:* 4-6 miles easy [6-10 km.].

PM: 8-mile control (tempo) run at 5:00 per mile [13 km.].

Wed 17 *AM:* 4-6 miles easy [6-10 km.].

PM: Easy run (20-30 min.).

Thurs 18 *AM:* 4-6 miles easy [6-10 km.].

PM: (1) 1500 meters or mile Simulation Drill #1; progress toward Drill #11.

(2) 30-minute run.

Fri 19 *AM:* Easy run (20-30 min.).

PM: Easy run (20-30 min.).

Sat 20 *AM:* Easy run (20-30 min.).

PM: (1) 1500 meters or mile Simulation Drill #2; progress toward Drill #12.

(2) 20-minute easy run.

(3) 3 × 800 cut-downs (70-66-62 pace for 400 meters), like this:

1 × 800 in 2:20, jog 200 meters.

1 × 800 in 2:12, jog 200 meters.

1 × 800 in 2:04, jog 200 meters.

Sun 21 12-15 miles at a comfortable pace [20-25 km.].

14-DAY COMPETITIVE PATTERN

Mon 1 *AM:* 3-7 miles easy [5-11 km.].

PM: (1) 40-minute fartlek run.

(2) 6-8×200 in 30 seconds with 30-second recoveries.

Tues 2 *AM:* 3-7 miles easy [5-11 km.].

PM: (1) 3 × 800 at 1500 meters or mile Goal Pace.

(2) 9×300 cut-downs (48-45-42) with 100-meter rests.

(3) Easy run on grass or other soft surface.

Wed 3 *AM:* 3-7 miles easy [5-11 km.].

PM: 40-minute easy run.

Thurs 4 *AM:* 3-7 miles easy [5-11 km.].

PM: (1) Intervals at 1500 meters or mile Goal

(continued)		Pace, run like this:

1 × 400 at Goal Pace, jog 200 meters.
1 × 600 at Goal Pace, jog 200 meters.
1 × 400 at Goal Pace, jog 200 meters.
1 × 200 at Goal Pace, jog 200 meters.
(2) 30-minute run.

Fri 5 *AM:* Easy run (20-30 min.).
PM: Easy run (20-30 min.).

Sat 6 *AM:* Easy run on grass or other soft surface.
PM: Race: Might vary from 800 to 5000 meters.

Sun 7 12-mile run [20 km.].

Mon 8 *AM:* 3-7 miles easy [5-11 km.].
PM: (1) 45-minute fartlek run.
(2) 4 × 150 sprint-float-sprint.
Accelerate for 50 meters.
Float for 50 meters.
Accelerate for 50 meters.

Tues 9 *AM:* 3-7 miles easy [5-11 km.].
PM: (1) Intervals at 1500 meters or mile Goal Pace.
1 × 400 at Goal Pace, jog 200 meters.
1 × 600 at Goal Pace, jog 200 meters.
1 × 400 at Goal Pace, jog 200 meters.
1 × 200 at Goal Pace, jog 200 meters.
(2) 2-4 × 600-meter set cut-downs; 1 set equals:
1 × 600 at 75 seconds for 400 pace, jog 200 meters.
1 × 500 at 70 seconds for 400 pace, jog 200 meters.
1 × 400 in 65 seconds, jog 200 meters.
1 × 300 in 45 seconds, jog 200 meters.
1 × 200 in 28 seconds, jog 100 meters.
1 × 100 in 13 seconds, jog 100 meters.

Wed 10 *AM:* 3-7 miles easy [5-11 km.].
PM: 5-7 miles at a comfortable pace [8-11 km.].

Thurs 11 *AM:* 3-7 miles easy [5-11 km.].
PM: (1) 3 × 400 in 55 seconds with 400-meter rests.
(2) 20-minute run.

(continued)   (3) 3 × 300 cut-downs (48-45-42), with 100-meter jogs.

Fri   **12**   *AM:* Easy run (20-30 min.).

PM: Easy run (20-30 min.).

Sat   **13**   *AM:* Easy run (20-30 min.).

PM: Race.

Sun   **14**   8-12 miles [13-20 km.].

10-DAY CHAMPIONSHIP PATTERN

Thurs   **1**   *AM:* 5-7 miles easy [8-11 km.].

PM: (1) 4 × 800 with 400-meter rests. Run 2 seconds slower per 400 meters than Goal Pace.

(2) 4 × 400 at Goal Pace with 300-meter rests.

(3) 4 × 200 with 100-meter rests. Run 2 seconds per 200 meters faster than Goal Pace.

Fri   **2**   *AM:* Easy run (20-30 min.) on grass or other soft surface.

PM: Easy run (20-30 min.) on grass or other soft surface.

Sat   **3**   *AM:* Easy run (20-30 min.) on grass or other soft surface.

PM: (1) 800 trial at full effort.

(2) 5 miles at a comfortable pace [8 km.].

(3) 5 × 300 cut-downs with 100 rests.

Sun   **4**   *AM:* Easy run (20-30 min.) on grass or other surface.

PM: Easy run (20-30 min.) on grass or other soft surface.

Mon   **5**   *AM:* 3-7 miles easy [5-11 km.].

PM: (1) 30-minute run at a comfortable pace.

(2) 6 × 200 in 30 seconds with 30 seconds for recoveries.

Tues   **6**   *AM:* 3-6 miles easy [5-10 km.].

PM: (1) 3 × 400 in 52-54 seconds with 300-meter rests.

(2) Easy run (20-30 min.) on grass or other soft surface.

Wed 7   *AM:* Easy run (20-30 min.) on grass or other soft surface.

      PM: (1) Easy run (20-30 min.) on grass or other soft surface.

      (2) 3-5 striders (80-100 meters) on grass or other soft surface.

Thurs 8   *AM:* Easy run (20-30 min.) on grass or other soft surface.

      PM: Trial Heats: 1500 meters.

Fri 9   *AM:* Easy run (20-30 min.) on grass or other soft surface.

      PM: Semifinals, if necessary. If no race, easy run on grass or other soft surface.

Sat 10   Finals in 1500 meters.

5000- and 10,000-Meter Run Training

These workouts are designed for national- to international-level college-age male athletes who run or desire to run under 13:45 for 5000 meters or under 29:00 for 10,000 meters. You should keep this in mind as you design your own training based on this pattern. Any running times should be scaled to your own level of ability and experience, rather than trying to do these exact workouts.

21-DAY PRE-SEASON PATTERN

Mon 1   *AM:* 5-8 miles easy [8-13 km.].

      PM: (1) 60-minute fartlek run.

      (2) 6×200 in 30 seconds with 30-second recoveries.

Tues 2   *AM:* 5-8 miles easy [8-13 km.].

      PM: 12-mile control (tempo) run at 5:20-5:30 per mile [20 km.].

Wed 3   *AM:* 5-8 miles easy [8-13 km.].

      PM: 40-minute easy run.

Thurs 4   *AM:* 5-8 miles easy [8-13 km.].

      PM: (1) Intervals at 1500 meters or mile Goal Pace.

      1×400 at Goal Pace, 200-400 meter jogs.

      1×600 at Goal Pace, 200-400 meter jogs.

10,000 meters. The ultimate test of speed and endurance on the track is a race Craig Virgin has mastered. Herb Lindsay hung on for four miles before Virgin said goodbye at the 1980 Olympic Trials.

(continued)   1 × 400 at Goal Pace, 200-400 meter jogs.
1 × 200 at Goal Pace, 200-400 meter jogs.
Use 400-meter jogs when you begin, gradually reducing the rest intervals to 200 meters as your condition improves.
(2) 30-minute run.
(3) 6 × 300 cut-downs with 100-meter rests.

Fri   **5**   *AM:* Easy run (20-30 min.).
         PM: Easy run (20-30 min.).

Sat   **6**   *AM:* Easy run (20-30 min.).
         PM: 10-mile run at 5:00 per mile [16 km.].

Sun   **7**   15 miles at a comfortable pace [25 km.].

Mon   **8**   *AM:* 5-8 miles easy [8-13 km.].
         PM: (1) 45-minute fartlek run.
               (2) 8 × 200 in 30 seconds with 30-second recoveries.

Tues   **9**   *AM:* 5-8 miles easy [8-13 km.].
         PM: 10-mile run at 5:20 per mile [16 km.].

Wed   **10**   *AM:* 5-8 miles easy [8-13 km.].
         PM: Easy run (20-30 min.).

Thurs   **11**   *AM:* 5-8 miles easy [8-13 km.].
         PM: (1) 1 mile [1600 meters] at Date Pace.
               (2) 4 miles (16 laps) at 80 seconds per 400 meter pace.

Fri   **12**   *AM:* Easy run (20-30 min.).
         PM: Easy run (20-30 min.).

Sat   **13**   *AM:* Easy run (20-30 min.).
         PM: (1) 6 × 800 at 5000 meters Goal Pace with 400-meter rests.
               (2) 5-mile run [8 km.].

Sun   **14**   15 miles at a comfortable pace [25 km.].

Mon   **15**   *AM:* 5-8 miles easy [8-13 km.].
         PM: (1) 45-minute fartlek.
               (2) 10 × 200 in 30 seconds with 30-second recoveries.

Tues   **16**   *AM:* 5-8 miles easy [8-13 km.].
         PM: 12-mile control (tempo) run at 5:20-5:30 per mile [20 km.].

Wed   **17**   *AM:* 4-8 miles easy [6-13 km.].

(continued) PM: 5-8 miles easy [8-13 km.].

Thurs 18 *AM:* 4-8 miles easy [6-13 km.].

PM: (1) 2-3 (8-12 laps) miles of 40/30 drill. Alternate 200s of 40 seconds, followed by 30 seconds, followed by 40 seconds, and so on, totaling 70 seconds per 400 meters. When you cannot continue the pace, stop the workout.

(2) Easy run (20-30 min.) on grass or other soft surface.

Fri 19 *AM:* Easy run (20-30 min.).

PM: Easy run (20-30 min.).

Sat 20 *AM:* Easy run (20-30 min.).

PM: (1) 10,000 meters Simulation Drill.

(2) Easy run (20-30 min.).

Sun 21 12-15 miles at a comfortable pace [20-25 km.].

14-DAY COMPETITIVE PATTERN

Mon 1 *AM:* 5-7 miles easy [8-11 km.].

PM: (1) 40-minute fartlek run.

(2) 6×200 in 30 seconds with 30-second recoveries.

Tues 2 *AM:* 5-7 miles easy [8-11 km.].

PM: (1) 6×800 at 5000 meters Date Pace, 200-meter jogs.

(2) 20-minute run on grass or other soft surface.

(3) 3×300 cut-downs, 100-meter jogs.

Wed 3 *AM:* 5-7 miles easy [8-11 km.].

PM: 40-minute steady run.

Thurs 4 *AM:* 5-7 miles easy [8-11 km.].

PM: (1) 6×300 in 45 seconds or Goal Pace for 1500 meters or mile, with 100-meter jog.

(2) 30-minute run on grass or other soft surface.

Fri 5 *AM:* 5 miles easy [8 km.].

PM: 20-30 min. run on grass or other soft surface.

Sat 6 *AM:* Easy run (20-30 min.) on grass or other soft surface.

(continued) PM: Race: 5000 or 1500 meters; switch distance the next week.

Sun   **7**   12 miles at a comfortable pace [20 km.].

Mon   **8**   *AM:* 5-8 miles easy [8-13 km.].

          PM: (1) 60-minute fartlek run.

               (2) 6×200 in 30 seconds with 30-second recoveries.

Tues   **9**   *AM:* 5-8 miles easy [8-13 km.].

          PM: (1) Intervals at 1500 meters or mile Goal Pace.

               1×400 at Goal Pace, jog 200 meters.

               1×600 at Goal Pace, jog 200 meters.

               1×400 at Goal Pace, jog 200 meters.

               1×200 at Goal Pace, jog 200 meters.

               (2) 2-4×600-meter set at 5000 meters Date Pace; 1 set equals:

               1×600 at Date Pace, jog 200 meters.

               1×400 at Date Pace, jog 200 meters.

               1×300 at Date Pace, jog 200 meters.

               1×200 at Date Pace, jog 100 meters.

               1×100 at Date Pace, jog 100 meters.

Wed   **10**   *AM:* 5-8 miles easy [8-13 km.].

          PM: 5-8 miles easy [8-13 km.].

Thurs **11**   *AM:* 5-8 miles easy [8-13 km.].

          PM: (1) 4 miles (16 laps) on track (no spikes). Run at 75-80 seconds pace per 400 meters.

               (2) Easy run (20-30 min.) on grass or other soft surface (cooldown).

Fri   **12**   *AM:* 5-mile run [8 km.].

          PM: 20-30 min. run on grass or other soft surface.

Sat   **13**   *AM:* Easy run (20-30 min.).

          PM: Race; either 1500, 5000 or 10,000.

Sun   **14**   12 miles easy [20 km.].

10-DAY CHAMPIONSHIP PATTERN

Thurs **1**   *AM:* 5-8 miles easy [8-13 km.].

          PM: (1) 4×1200 at 5000 meters Goal Pace with 800-meter rests.

               (2) 3×mile [1600] cut-downs, such as 5:00-

(continued)   4:40-4:26. Jog 400 meters after each.
                       (3) Easy run (20-30 min.) on grass or other
                       soft surface.

Fri **2** *AM:* Easy run (20-30 min.) on grass or other soft
                       surface.

            PM: Easy run (20-30 min.) on grass or other
                       surface.

Sat **3** *AM:* Easy run (20-30 min.) on grass or other soft
                       surface.

            PM: (1) Mile or 1600 at Date Pace.
                       (2) 2 × 600 meter sets at 5000 meters Date
                       Pace; 1 set equals:
                       1 × 600 at Date Pace, 200-meter rest.
                       1 × 400 at Date Pace, 200-meter rest.
                       1 × 300 at Date Pace, 100-meter rest.
                       1 × 200 at Date Pace, 100-meter rest.
                       1 × 100 at Date Pace, 100-meter rest.
                       (3) Easy run (20-30 min.) on grass or other
                       soft surface.

Sun **4** 12-15 miles at a comfortable pace [20-25 km.].

Mon **5** *AM:* 5-8 miles easy [8-13 km.].
                11:00 AM: (2) 2 × 200 in 26 seconds, with
                200-meter recovery jogs.
                       (2) One mile of running on grass or other soft
                       surface.

            PM: 5 miles of easy running [8 km.].

Tues **6** *AM:* 5-8 miles easy [8-13 km.].
            PM: (1) 4 miles (16 laps) at 75-80 seconds for 400
                       meters.
                       (2) 3 × 300 cut-downs (50-47-44) with
                       100-meter rests.

Wed **7** *AM:* 2-4 miles easy running [3-7 km.].
            PM: 30 minutes easy running on grass or other
                       soft surface.

Thurs **8** *AM:* Easy run (20-30 min.) on grass or other soft
                       surface.

            PM: Qualifying Heats.

Fri **9** 20-minute easy run on grass or other soft
                surface.

Sat 10 *AM:* Easy run (20-30 min.) on grass or other soft surface.

   PM: Race Final.

The 5000-Meter Simulation Drills
(Used in 5000-10,000 training pattern):

5000 Simulation Drill #1: Run 12 laps [3 miles or 4800 meters] like this: Alternate running a 400 at Goal Pace, followed by an 800 at 80-90 seconds for 400 meters.

First 400 at Goal Pace	Lap 1.
Next 800 at 80-90 seconds for 400 meters	Laps 2-3.
Next 400 at Goal Pace	Lap 4.
Next 800 at 80-90 seconds for 400 meters pace	Laps 5-6.
Next 400 at Goal Pace	Lap 7.
Next 800 at 80-90 seconds for 400 meters pace	Laps 8-9.
Next 400 at Goal Pace	Lap 10.
Last 800 at 80-90 seconds for 400 meters pace	Laps 11-12.

5000 Simulation Drill #2: Run 12 laps [3 miles or 4800 meters] like this: Alternate running an 800 at Goal Pace, followed by 3 laps at 80-90 seconds for 400 meters pace:

First 800 at Goal Pace	Laps 1-2.
Next 3 laps at 80-90 seconds for 400 meters pace	Laps 3-5.
Middle 800 at Goal Pace	Laps 6-7.
Next 3 laps at 80-90 seconds for 400 meters pace	Laps 8-10.
Last 800 at Goal Pace	Laps 11-12.

5000 Simulation Drill #3: Run 12 laps [3 miles or 4800 meters] like this:

First 1 km. [2½ laps] at Goal Pace	Laps 1-2.5.
Next 800 (2 laps) at 80-90 seconds for 400 meters pace	Laps 2.5-4.5.
Next 1 km. (2½ laps) at Goal Pace	Laps 4.5-7.
Next 800 (2 laps) at 80-90 seconds for 400 meters pace	Laps 8-9.
Last 1200 (3 laps) at Goal Pace	Laps 10-12.

5000 Simulation Drill #4: Run 12 laps [3 miles or 4800 meters] like this:

First 3 laps at Goal Pace	Laps 1-3.
Next 3 laps at 80-90 seconds for 400 meters pace	Laps 4-6.

Next 3 laps at Goal Pace   Laps 7-9.

Last 3 laps at 80-90 seconds for 400 meters pace

                                                    Laps 10-12.

Alternate Version:

First 3 laps at 80-90 seconds for 400 meters pace   Laps 1-3.

Next 3 laps at Goal Pace   Laps 4-6.

Next 3 laps at 80-90 seconds for 400 meters pace   Laps 7-9.

Last 3 laps at Goal Pace   Laps 10-12.

5000 Simulation Drill #5: Run 12 laps [3 miles or 4800 meters] like this:

First 3 laps at Goal Pace   Laps 1-3.

Next 2 laps at 80-90 seconds for 400 meters pace

                                                     Laps 4-5.

Middle 2 laps at Goal Pace   Laps 6-7.

Next 2 laps at 80-90 seconds for 400 meters pace

                                                     Laps 8-9.

Last 3 laps at Goal Pace   Laps 10-12.

5000 Simulation Drill #6: Run 12 laps [3 miles or 4800 meters] like this:

First 3 laps at Goal Pace   Laps 1-3.

Next 600 at 80-90 seconds for 400 meters pace

                                                 Laps 4-5.5.

Middle 3 laps at Goal Pace   Laps 5.5-8.5.

Next 600 at 80-90 seconds for 400 meters pace

                                                 Laps 8.5-9.

Last 3 laps at Goal Pace   Laps 10-12.

The 10,000-Meter Simulation Drills
(Used in 5000-10,000 training pattern):

10,000 Simulation Drill #1: Run 24 laps [6 miles or 9600 meters] like this:

Repeat this pattern for 24 laps:

400 meters at Goal Pace.

400 meters in 80-90 seconds.

Total: 12 cycles.

10,000 Simulation Drill #2: Run 24 laps [6 miles or 9600 meters] like this:

Repeat this pattern for 24 laps:

800 meters (2 laps) at Goal Pace.

400 meters in 80-90 seconds.
Total: 8 cycles.

10,000 Simulation Drill #3: Run 25 laps [6.25 miles or 10 km.] like this:
Repeat this pattern for 25 laps:
3 laps (1200 meters) at Goal Pace.
2 laps (800 meters) at 80-90 seconds for 400 meters pace.
Total: 5 cycles.

10,000 Simulation Drill #4: Run 24 laps [6 miles or 9600 meters] like this:
Repeat this pattern for 24 laps:
4 laps (1600 meters) at Goal Pace.
2 laps (800 meters) at 80-90 seconds for 400 meters pace.
Total: 4 cycles.

10,000 Simulation Drill #5: Run 26 laps [6.5 miles or 10,400 meters] like this:

4 laps at Goal Pace	Laps 1-4.
Next 600 at 90 seconds for 400 meters pace	Laps 5-6.5.
4 laps at Goal Pace	Laps 6.5-10.5.
Next 600 at 90 seconds for 400 meters pace	Laps 10.5-11.
Middle 4 laps at Goal Pace	Laps 12-15.
Next 600 at 90 seconds for 400 meters pace	Laps 16-17.5.
Next 4 laps at Goal Pace	Laps 17.5-21.5.
Next 600 at 90 seconds for 400 meters pace	Laps 21.5-22.
Last 4 laps at Goal Pace	Laps 23-26.

10,000 Simulation Drill #6: Run 24 laps [6 miles or 9600 meters] like this:

First 4 laps at Goal Pace	Laps 1-4.
Next 400 in 80-90 seconds	Lap 5.
Next 4 laps at Goal Pace	Laps 6-9.
Next 400 in 80-90 seconds	Lap 10.
Middle 4 laps at Goal Pace	Laps 11-14.
Next 400 in 80-90 seconds	Lap 15.
Next 4 laps at Goal Pace	Laps 16-19.
Next 400 in 80-90 seconds	Lap 20.
Last 4 laps at Goal Pace	Laps 21-24.

Marathon Training

These workouts are designed for a national- to international-level male athlete who runs or desires to run under 2:15 for the marathon. You should keep this in mind as you design your own training based on this pattern. Any running times should be scaled to your own level of ability and experience, rather than trying to do these workouts exactly as they appear.

21-DAY OFF-SEASON PATTERN

Each time you repeat the 21-day pattern, the pattern will remain basically the same, but the workouts should become progressively harder. The following changes can be made in specific workouts:

Day 1: Remains basically the same.

Day 3: Every other week will be a fartlek run. Add time to the run until you reach two hours of fartlek. After reaching two hours, drop back to one hour and begin increasing the time again. The intensity of your training will have increased as your strength and endurance have increased.

Day 7: The mile time should gradually be lowered as you improve.

Day 10: Gradually increase your mileage until you reach either 24 miles or three hours (whichever comes first) of running at a steady pace.

Day 14: Gradually cut the mile down to 4:40 and the rest times to 5:20. This is a 9-mile continuous run, alternating fast and slow miles, with the first, third, fifth, seventh and ninth miles at the fast pace.

Sun 1 *AM:* Long, easy run — about 15 miles at a steady pace.

Mon 2 *AM:* Easy run (20-30 min.).
PM: Easy run (20-30 min.).

Tues 3 *AM:* 7-10 mile run [12-16 km.].
PM: One hour varied fartlek run.

Wed   **4**   *AM:* Easy run (20-30 min.).
            PM: Easy run (20-30 min.).
Thurs **5**   *AM:* 7-10 mile run [12-16 km.].
            PM: 7-10 mile run [12-16 km.].
Fri   **6**   *AM:* Easy run (20-30 min.).
            PM: Easy run (20-30 min.).
Sat   **7**   *AM:* 6 × mile at 10 seconds per mile faster than marathon pace. Take 440-yard recovery jogs.
            PM: 5-8 mile run [8-13 km.].
Sun: **8**   *AM:* Easy run (20-30 min.).
            PM: Easy run (20-30 min.).
Mon   **9**   *AM:* Easy run (20-30 min.).
            PM: Easy run (20-30 min.).
Tues **10** *Noon:* 18-mile run [30 km.] at an even pace.
Wed **11** *AM:* Easy run (20-30 min.).
            PM: Easy run (20-30 min.).
Thurs 12 *AM:* 5-8 mile run [8-13 km.].
            PM: 5-8 mile run [8-13 km.].
Fri   **13** *AM:* Easy run (20-30 min.).
            PM: Easy run (20-30 min.).
Sat   **14** *AM:* 9 × in-and-out miles. Example: 5:00—5:30—5:00—5:30—5:00—5:30—5:00—5:30—5:00
Sun   **15** *AM:* Easy run (20-30 min.).
            PM: Easy run (20-30 min.).
Mon **16** *AM:* Easy run (20-30 min.).
            PM: Easy run (20-30 min.).
Tues **17** *AM:* 1½ hours of varied fartlek.
            PM: 5 miles easy running [8 km.].
Wed **18** *AM:* Easy run (20-30 min.).
            PM: Easy run (20-30 min.).
Thurs 19 *AM:* 7-10 mile run [12-16 km.].
            PM: 7-10 mile run [12-16 km.].
Fri   **20** *AM:* Easy run (20-30 min.).
            PM: Easy run (20-30 min.).
Sat   **21** *AM:* 5 × 880-330 drill cut-downs. Run an 880, jog a 220, run a 330, jog a 330, then start over again: 2:40—54 seconds; 2:35—52 seconds; 2:30—50 seconds; 2:24—48 seconds; 2:20—46 seconds.
            PM: 5-mile run [8 km.].

10-DAY CHAMPIONSHIP PATTERN

Fri 1 *PM:* Simulated Surging Drill (This is a continuous running drill). Run 8¾ miles (14 km.) like this: One mile in 4:40; 3 miles at 5:00 pace (15:00—total time of 19:40); ¾ mile in 3:18-3:24 (total time of 22:58-23:04); 3 miles at 5:00 pace (15:00—total time of 37:58-38:04); One mile in 4:30 (total time of 42:28-42:34).

Sat 2 *AM:* 5-7 mile run [8-12 km.].
PM: 5-7 mile run [8-12 km.].

Sun 3 *AM:* 7-10 mile run [12-16 km.].
PM: 7-10 mile run [12-16 km.].

Mon 4 *AM:* 5 miles [8 km.] on the track at 4:50-5:00 pace per mile.
PM: 7-10 mile [12-16 km.] easy run.

Tues 5 *AM:* 5-mile [8 km.] easy run.
PM: 5-mile [8 km.] run. 5×330 yards in 48 seconds, with 110-yard recovery jogs.

Wed 6 *AM:* 5-8 mile [8-13 km.] run.
PM: 5-8 mile [8-13 km.] run.

Thurs 7 *10:00 AM:* 4×880-330 drill. Run an 880, jog a 220, run a 330, jog a 330, then start over again. 2:40—52 seconds; 2:30—50 seconds; 2:20—48 seconds; 2:10—46 seconds.
PM: Easy run (20-30 min.).

Fri 8 *AM:* 5-mile [8 km.] run.
PM: 5-mile [8 km.] run.

Sat 9 *Noon:* Easy 5-mile [8 km.] run.

Sun 10 Competition.

Steeplechase Training

These workouts are designed for national- to international-level college-age male athletes who run or desire to run under 8:40 for the 3000-meter steeplechase. You should keep this in mind as you design your own training based on this pattern. Any running times should be scaled to your own level of ability and experience, rather than trying to do these exact workouts.

Steeplechase. Water jumps and barriers make this 3000-meter event a test of endurance and leaping ability. Doug Brown leads in the 1980 Olympic Trials before fading to second.

21-DAY PRE-SEASON PATTERN

Mon **1** *AM:* 30-minute run.

PM: (1) Hurdle technique instruction. Steps #1 and #2 of hurdle progression.

(2) 40-minute fartlek run.

(3) 6×200 in 30 seconds with 30-second recoveries.

Tues **2** *AM:* 30-minute run.

PM: 10-mile steady run at a hard pace [16 km.]. Tempo should be difficult to maintain; workout should hurt a bit.

Wed 3   *AM:* 30-minute easy run.

    PM: (1) Hurdle technique instruction. Steps #1, #2, and #3 of hurdle progression.

    (2) 30-minute easy run.

Thurs 4   *AM:* 30-minute run.

    PM: (1) 5 × 300 at 1500 meters or mile Goal Pace with 300-meter rets.

    (2) 30-minute easy run.

Fri 5   *AM:* 30-minute run.

    PM: (1) Water jump technique instruction: Step #1.

    (2) Easy run (20-30 min.) on grass or other soft surface.

Sat 6   *AM:* Easy run (20-30 min.).

    PM: (1) 1 × mile or 1600 meters at Date Pace.

    (2) 7-10 miles at a good, steady pace.

    (3) 5 × 300 cut-downs with 100-meter rests. Begin with Date Pace and drop below Goal Pace by last 300.

Sun 7   12 miles at a comfortable pace [20 km.].

Mon 8   *AM:* 30-minute run.

    PM: (1) Hurdle drill #4.

    (2) 40-minute fartlek run.

    (3) 8 × 200 in 30 seconds with 30-second recoveries.

Tues 9   *AM:* 30-minute run.

    PM: (1) 3-5 × mile or 1600 at Date Pace with 800-meter rests.

    (2) Easy run (20-30 min.).

Wed 10   *AM:* 30-minute run.

    PM: (1) Hurdle drill #5.

    (2) 30-minute run.

Thurs 11   *AM:* 30-minute run.

    PM: (1) 5 × 400 at 1500 meters or mile Goal Pace with 300-meter rests.

    (2) Easy run (20-30 min.) on grass or other soft surface.

Fri 12   *AM:* Easy run (20-30 min.).

    PM: (1) Water jump progression Drills #2 and #3.

    (2) Easy run (20-30 min.).

Sat 13   *10:00 AM:* 12-mile control (tempo) run [20 km.].

(continued) Begin at a comfortable pace, then speed up every 2 miles; last 2 miles are at Date Pace for 1500 or mile.

P M :Easy run (20-30 min.).

Sun 14 12-15-miles at a comfortable pace [20-25 km.].

Mon 15 *AM:* 30-minute run.

PM: (1) Hurdle drill step #6.

(2) 30-minute fartlek run.

(3) 10 × 200 in 30 seconds with 30-second recoveries.

Tues 16 *AM:* 30-minute run.

PM: 10-mile run at a hard, steady pace (each mile timed) [16 km.].

Wed 17 *AM:* 30-minute run.

PM: (1) Water jump progression step #4.

(2) Easy run (20-30 min.) on grass or other soft surface.

Thurs 18 *AM:* 30-minute run.

PM: 4 miles (16 laps) on track at half-effort, with intermediate hurdles at the 4 steeplechase barrier marks.

Fri 19 *AM:* Easy run (20-30 min.).

PM: Easy run (20-30 min.).

Sat 20 *10:00 AM:* (1) 2 miles [3200 meters] race simulation. First 2 laps over hurdles at Goal Pace. Run over 4 intermediate hurdles per lap. Middle 4 laps on flat at 80-90 seconds for 400 meters. Last 2 laps over hurdles at Goal Pace.

(2) 30-40 min. run.

Sun 21 12-15 miles at a comfortable pace [20-25 km.].

14-DAY COMPETITIVE PATTERN

Mon 1 *AM:* 5-7 miles [8-11 km.].

PM: (1) 45-minute fartlek run.

(2) 6 × 200 in 28 seconds with 32-second recoveries.

Tues 2 *AM:* 5-7 miles [8-11 km.].

PM: (1) 2 × 1200 at 5000 meters Goal Pace with 600-meter rests.

(2) 2 × 800 at 3000 meters Goal Pace with

(continued) 400-meter rests.

(3) 2 × 400 at 1500 meters Goal Pace with 300-meter rests.

(4) Easy run (20-30 min.) on grass or other soft surface.

Wed   **3**   *AM:* 5-7 miles [8-11 km.].

PM: (1) 4 × 200 over 2 intermediate hurdles set at barrier marks. Jog 200 meters for recovery after each fast 200.

(2) 7-mile steady run [11 km.].

Thurs **4**   *AM:* 5-7 miles [8-11 km.].

PM: (1) 3 × 400 at Goal Pace for 1500 meters or mile with 200-meter rests.

(2) 30-minute easy run.

Fri   **5**   *AM:* 5 miles easy [8 km.].

PM: 5 miles easy [8 km.].

Sat   **6**   *Flat Race:* 1500 or 5000 meters: overdistance or underdistance.

Sun   **7**   8-12 miles at a comfortable pace [13-20 km.].

Mon   **8**   *AM:* 5-7 miles easy [8-11 km.].

PM: 45-minute fartlek run.

Tues   **9**   *AM:* 5-7 miles easy [8-11 km.].

PM: (1) Intervals at 1500 meters or mile Goal Pace with 200-300 meter rests.

1 × 400 at Goal Pace, jog 200-300 meters.

1 × 600 at Goal Pace, jog 200-300 meters.

1 × 400 at Goal Pace, jog 200-300 meters.

1 × 200 at Goal Pace, jog 200-300 meters.

(2) 30-minutes steady run.

Wed   **10**   *AM:* 5-7 miles easy [8-11 km.].

PM: (1) 4 × water jump with pit covered by plywood.

(2) 7 miles at a steady pace [11 km.].

Thurs **11**   *AM:* 5-7 miles easy [8-11 km.].

PM: (1) 2 miles at 80 seconds pace for 400 meters over hurdles. Set intermediate hurdles at each barrier location [4].

(2) Easy run (20-30 min.) on grass or other soft surface.

Fri 12 *AM:* Easy run (20-30 min.) on grass or other soft surface.

PM: Easy run (20-30 min.) on grass or other soft surface.

Sat 13 *Race:* Steeplechase.

Sun 14 8-12 miles easy [13-20 km.].

10-DAY CHAMPIONSHIP PATTERN

Thurs 1 *AM:* 5-7 miles easy [8-11 km.].

PM: (1) 3 × 400 in 55-57 seconds with 300-meter rests.

(2) 20-minute run on grass or other soft surface.

(3) 3 × 300 cut-downs in 49-46-43 with 100-meter rests.

Fri 2 *AM:* Easy run (20-30 min.) on grass or other soft surface.

PM: Easy run (20-30 min.) on grass or other soft surface.

Sat 3 *AM:* Easy run (20-30 min.) on grass or other soft surface.

PM: (1) 2 × mile or 1600 at pick-up tempo. First 400 at steeplechase Goal Pace, with each lap faster than the lap before, and lap #4 at 1500 meters or mile Goal Pace. Example: 67-65-63-59 = 4:14-4:16. 1200 meters (3 laps) recovery between.

(2) Easy run (20-30 min.) on grass or other soft surface.

Sun 4 *AM:* Easy run (20-30 min.).

PM: Easy run (20-30 min.).

Mon 5 *AM:* 5-7 miles easy [8-11 km.].

PM: 40-minute fartlek run.

Tues 6 *AM:* 5-7 miles easy [8-11 km.].

PM: (1) Intervals at 1500 meters or mile Goal Pace.

1 × 400 at Goal Pace, jog 200 meters.

1 × 600 at Goal Pace, jog 200 meters.

1 × 400 at Goal Pace, jog 200 meters.

(continued) 1 × 200 at Goal Pace, jog 200 meters.
(2) Easy run (20-30 min.) on grass or other soft surface.
(3) 3 × 300 cut-downs (50-47-43) with 100-meter rests.

Wed 7 *AM:* Easy run (20-30 min.) on grass or other soft surface.

PM: Easy run (20-30 min.) on grass or other soft surface.

Thurs 8 *AM:* Easy run (20-30 min.) on grass or other soft surface.

PM: Qualifying Heats, if necessary. If no heats:
(1) 8 × 200 in 30 seconds, 200-meter jogs.
(2) Easy run (20-30 min.) on grass or other soft surface.

Fri 9 *AM:* Easy run (20-30 min.) on grass or other soft surface.

PM: Easy run (20-30 min.) on grass or other soft surface.

Sat 10 Race Final.

The Steeplechase Progression Steps

Hurdle technique progression. These are the steps used at Oregon to introduce distance runners to the hurdles and the techniques they will need to clear the barriers in a steeplechase. The special training usually begins in December, after cross-country season has ended.

Step 1: Approach a low hurdle (30 inches or 76 cm.), stepping with your trail leg to the side and about two feet (60 cm.) behind the hurdle, lifting your lead knee, then stepping past the hurdle while bringing your trail leg through to the side in the normal hurdling motion. With the trail leg, your knee should come out to the side and your trailing toe should be turned out and up to avoid hitting the hurdle. With your lead leg, always lift the knee first (bent, not straight), then reach for the hurdle with your foot. Step 1 just calls for going past the hurdle to the side, with no clearance of the hurdle.

Step 2: Jog to the hurdle and step past it as if you were hurdling, but bring your trail leg over the hurdle (your lead leg will pass beside the hurdle, clearing open air).

Step 3: Jog to the hurdle and step over the hurdle with both your lead leg and your trail leg.

Step 4: Take six hurdles and place them on two alternating lanes of the track straightaway, such as lanes 5 and 7. Have three hurdles in each lane, set about 20 to 25 yards (or meters) apart, with those in one lane facing in one direction, and those in the other lane facing in the other direction, so you can run the hurdles both going and returning. Jog the straightaway, clearing the hurdles with alternating lead legs. Gradually slow down after the third hurdle, then turn around and return on the other lane with hurdles, running in the same manner as before.

Step 5: This is the same drill as in step 4, but the hurdles are raised from 30 inches to the normal steeplechase height of 36 inches (91 cm.).

Step 6: Practice setting a marker about 13 yards (12 meters) from the hurdle, and learn to accelerate your last few strides to the hurdle. This makes it easier to approach a barrier ready to go with your preferred lead leg, rather than staggering or shortening your stride just before the barrier.

In the hurdling drills, you should work on accelerating into the barrier, a low hurdle clearance, rhythm, balance and relaxation.

Water jump technique progression. Mastering the water jump requires courage as well as skill. You will jump from the top of a three-foot barrier into a rather imposing water-filled pit. You should land on one foot and try to leap as far forward as possible to clear the pit and maintain forward momentum. Trampoline activities are recommended: jumping for 15 to 20 minutes twice a week with bouncing and simple stunts like seat drops, front drops and back drops, which promote balance, body awareness and leg strength.

Step 1: Learn to hit a marker about 13 yards out and accelerate to a mark from which you will jump over a puddle or another mark, simulating jumping a creek or a water jump. At Oregon we do this twice a week for two weeks, practicing jumping off both feet (switching feet) to prepare for adjusting stride to the water jump.

Step 2: A log or box about 12 inches (30 cm.) high is used as a starting platform for jumps over the imaginary water jump. A target 10 to 12 feet (3 to 4 meters) past the box makes a landing zone. This is best done on grass or into a long jump pit.

Step 3: A thicker log or higher box is used for the same drill as in Step 2, raising the takeoff point to about 24 inches (60 cm.). Continue to practice the drill for two to four weeks. With this higher takeoff, only a soft landing surface should be used.

Step 4: A standard 36-inch (91 cm.) steeplechase barrier is placed at the end of a long jump runway on the edge of the landing pit. Run down the runway at about 70-seconds-per-400-meters speed, hitting your marker about 12 meters before the barrier. Accelerate from the marker, jumping onto the top of the barrier with one foot, then pushing off the other side, using your toes to push. Land in the pit near a 12-foot marker on your other foot, striding smoothly out of the pit without breaking your stride. The whole process—acceleration/take-off/landing—should be smooth and precise.

Use spikes for traction. Land atop the barrier with your toes over the far edge, then pivot across the top of the barrier and dig in against the far side with your spikes as you push off. If you push off too soon, you will gain height but not distance, and fall deeper into the sloping pit. The leap should be a low, continuous gliding movement across the top of the barrier.

Step 5: This step is much like Step 4, except that the water jump is used, although the surface is covered with plywood. At this point, you will run some intervals, which include hurdles and the covered water jump.

Step 6: This is the last stage, with the water jump uncovered and filled with water. Practicing will reduce your fear of the barriers and water jump. This type of practice should not be done too often, however, because of the stress on your legs and feet.

The Steeplechase Simulation Drills
(Used in the steeplechase training pattern):

Steeplechase Simulation Drill #1: Run 7.5 laps [3000 meters] like this:

First 400 over barriers and water jump at Goal Pace.
Middle 5½ laps on the flat at 80 seconds for 400 meters.
Last 400 over barriers and water jump at Goal Pace.

Steeplechase Simulation Drill #2: Run 7.5 laps [3000 meters] like this:

> First 600 over barriers and water jump at Goal Pace.
>
> Middle 4½ laps on the flat at 80 seconds for 400 meters.
>
> Last 600 over barriers and water jump at Goal Pace.

Steeplechase Simulation Drill #3: Run 7.5 laps [3000 meters] like this:

> First 400 over barriers and water jump at Goal Pace.
>
> Next 800 on the flat at 80 seconds for 400 meters.
>
> Next 600 over barriers and water jump at Goal Pace.
>
> Next 800 on the flat at 80 seconds for 400 meters.
>
> Last 400 over barriers and water jump at Goal Pace.

Steeplechase Simulation Drill #4: Run 7.5 laps [3000 meters] like this:

> First 800 over barriers and water jump at Goal Pace.
>
> Middle 3½ laps on the flat at 80 seconds for 400 meters.
>
> Last 800 over barriers and water jump at Goal Pace.

Steeplechase Simulation Drill #5: Run 8 laps [3200 meters] like this:

> First 800 on the flat at 80 seconds for 400 meters.
>
> Middle 4 laps over barriers and water jump at Goal Pace.
>
> Last 800 on the flat at 80 seconds for 400 meters.

Steeplechase Simulation Drill #6: Run 8 laps [3200 meters] like this:

> First 3 laps over barriers and water jump at Goal Pace.
>
> Middle 2 laps on the flat at 80 seconds for 400 meters.
>
> Last 3 laps over barriers and water jump at Goal Pace.

Steeplechase Simulation Drill #7: Run 8 laps [3200 meters] like this:

> First 2 laps over barriers and water jump at Goal Pace.
>
> Next 400 on the flat at 80 seconds for 400 meters.
>
> Middle 2 laps over barriers and water jump at Goal Pace.
>
> Next 400 on the flat at 80 seconds for 400 meters.
>
> Last 2 laps over barriers and water jump at Goal Pace.

10. Race Strategy

Successful racing isn't achieved just by having a good training program. To run your races well requires some knowledge of racing strategy or tactics. The most efficient way to run a race, and the way most likely to record your fastest time, is running at a steady pace. Each lap on the track or each kilometer or mile on the road is run at the same pace as the one before it.

Unfortunately, running a steady pace is not necessarily the way most likely to result in victory. When you are running only for a given time, or running to a set, steady pace is still the best way. But when you are running primarily to win, or simply competing against some friends, strategy enters the picture.

Although running a steady pace minimizes stress on the body, using this strategy all the time will help your opponents. If they know you are planning to run a certain pace, they can follow your lead, hoping to outkick you at the end of the race. Their chances to win are better, because it takes more energy to set and maintain a pace than it does to hold a pace set by someone else. Secondly, in poor weather if you set the pace and lead the whole way, you'll help those behind by allowing them to "draft." They'll save energy by letting you break the wind. Finally, with the other runners always behind you, you can't tell where they are or assess their physical state. They'll have a psychological edge.

If you are a well-prepared runner, you will have more than one weapon for your race plan. Many times you must wait for the race to develop before choosing your tactics. The opponent, weather, track conditions and your own feelings will dictate which tactics should be used. You should not use the same tactics in every race. Having a consistent racing strategy is the same as having no strategy at all, because your opponents will already know what you plan to do.

Let's look at some of the racing tactics you can use. The tactics are told by event, as each event has some peculiarities of its own.

TACTICS FOR THE 800 METERS

The following racing tactics are certainly not all there is, but they do offer a few suggestions for how you might run an 800-meter race. Obviously, you would not use all of these tactics in the same race.

(1) Having to run in the inside lane on an offset start (running in lanes around the first turn) can be a big disadvantage. As the runners come off the turn and break for the pole position, the runner in lane 1 can run into a box, with runners both in front and to the side. Once boxed, a runner has no way of moving up. If you are starting in lane 1, you should either:

    (a) accelerate around the turn, assuring yourself the lead when you reach the break point at the end of the turn, or

    (b) as you come off the turn and pass the break-line, ease outward into lane 2, giving yourself the length of the straightaway to move into the position you prefer.

(2) You can accelerate down the backstretch of the second lap of the race, beginning about 300 meters from the finish. You should then relax around the last turn, without losing speed. When you are challenged coming off the final turn, you should be ready to accelerate again. This is a skill learned by practicing the sprint-float-sprint (165 yards or 150 meters) drill.

(3) You should learn to sprint-float-sprint for 55 yards or 50 meters each. This skill is especially useful for your

drive off the turn and down the finishing straightaway.

(4)   If you are following the leader(s), you should never run directly behind another runner; instead, position yourself just outside, off his shoulder. When you are challenged and passed by another runner, pass the runner you were trailing and move into the same position next to the runner who passed you, trailing and just off his shoulder.

(5)   Avoid running too close to the curb in a track race. At the same time, you do not want to leave enough room for an opponent to pass on your inside. You should force your opponent to do the most work to pass you, while you have to do the least work to prevent being passed. You must use your best judgment, and you must be careful.

(6)   You should accelerate into the last turn, and then relax but carry your speed through the turn and into the final straightaway, accelerating over the last 55 yards or 50 meters.

(7)   If the wind is in your face on the backstretch of the last lap, let your opponent take the lead; he'll break the wind and shield you from it, saving you energy. You should pass the runner on the turn, taking the lead into the final straightaway with the wind to your back.

(8)   If the wind is against you on the final straightaway, take the lead going into the last turn. You will come off the turn in the lead, giving your opponent two challenges to meet: you and the head wind.

(9)   You should practice one-step accelerations (165-yard/-150-meter sprint-float-sprint drill). Pass your opponent, using quick acceleration for surprise, rather than slowly passing him. Remember: Quickness comes from shortening the stride for acceleration, rather than from lengthening the stride.

TACTICS FOR THE MILE AND 1500 METERS

The tactics used in the 1500 meters and mile run are very similar to those used in the 800 meters. The mile and 1500 meters are becoming more and more like "sprint" races, requiring great speed at the highest levels of competition. The tactics suggested for the 800 can also be used for the 1500 and mile. Or use these tactics:

(1) If you are racing against a faster opponent, start your drive or acceleration 600 to 660 yards (550 to 600 meters) from the finish, rather than waiting until late in the last lap of the race.

(2) The race is never won in the first 200 meters, so run your own pace over that part of the race. Most runners tend to start too fast and go into oxygen debt. Once you are in oxygen debt, your race might as well be over.

(3) Work on the third lap of your race. Most runners tend to relax three-quarters of the way into a race, regardless of its length. This mental lapse is very noticeable in the mile run. An experienced runner can win the race by forcing the pace on this lap, refusing to let the pace slow down.

TACTICS FOR THE 5000 AND 10,000 METERS

The 5000- and 10,000-meter races are long enough for you to use a variety of tactics. The tactics you use can depend upon many factors, such as the strengths and weaknesses of your opponent(s), the weather, and your personal strengths and weaknesses as a runner.

Remember that a tactic is not helpful unless you have calloused yourself to that particular move and your opponent has not prepared for it. Even if both of those conditions are true, you still have to get your opponent to respond to the tactic as you would expect.

Remember, the easiest way to run a fast time is at an even pace, whether you want to run 64 seconds per 400 meters for a 13:20 race at 5000 meters or 6:00 per mile (on a flat course) on the roads for a 37:17 at 10,000 meters. The length of race or level of your talent does not matter; even pace is the most efficient way to run. So if you are throwing in surges, but your opponent is catching up to you after each surge as he runs a steady pace, he is using less energy. Who do you think will win? Running steady pace during a race with a lot of surging enabled me to win the bronze medal at 5000 meters at the 1964 Olympic Games against runners with faster times.

The longer the race, the more time there is for runners to think. Use this time wisely and think ahead and it can work to your advantage. When running in a pack you have to stay alert for the inevitable jostling among runners. By the time the race is almost over, you may not have had time to think about your physical fatigue. You can gain an advantage at this time if you can break away from the pack by using your tactics.

Remember that the element of surprise is always going to enhance whatever tactic you use. Be imaginative; there are as many tactics as there are runners. These suggestions should give you ideas for others.

(1) Throw in a strong surge in the middle of the 5000 or 10,000 to try to break contact with your opponents. Once you have gotten a good lead, settle down to a steady pace. In most cases, your opponent will be defeated and unable to close the gap. If he stays with you when you surge, but has not trained himself to use this strategy, he risks losing his finishing strength or speed.

(2) If you are racing an opponent who you know has greater speed, make your final drive anywhere from three laps to 600 meters from the finish. Murray Halberg won the 1960 Olympic 5000 by throwing in a 58-second 400 with three laps remaining in the race. He gained 40 yards with this surprise move. Though his opponents closed the gap over the last two laps, he still finished seven meters ahead of the pack.

(3) Make a strong surge or pick up the pace while running into the wind, then relax down the other straightaway with the wind to your back.

(4) You should learn to sprint-float-sprint over the final 165 yards or 150 meters to the finish.

(5) Let your opponent get about 10 to 15 meters ahead of you and wait for the last 300 meters for your own surge. He may think he has broken contact with you and become careless and less alert to what you are doing.

(6) When you have the lead and are sprinting for the finish, run at about 95 percent effort, saving the last bit of strength to accept one more challenge. Stay relaxed and be ready to add the last 5 percent when it is needed.

TACTICS FOR THE MARATHON

The primary rule to remember about a marathon is that it is a very long race. You will be running for more than two hours, so you must be very patient. The most efficient way to run a marathon is at a steady pace, planning your race ahead of time.

Be sure to drink throughout the race, water being the best fluid. For the less experienced and the slower runners, water becomes more important to avoid dehydration. To play it safe, plan on taking water at every aid station during the marathon. Be sure you get water at the station; if you cannot drink while running, walk or stop and drink.

Your best tactic in a marathon is to stay in contact or within reach of your opponents for the first 17 to 21 miles [27 to 34 km.], making a race of it the last 10 kilometers. In his second marathon, Alberto Salazar (world record holder in the marathon) surged at 17 miles, trying to run his next three miles at 4:40 pace. Your tactics will depend upon your own strengths and weaknesses; Salazar cannot wait to kick at the end of the race against a runner with faster leg speed, so he must try to weaken him with surges or a faster pace earlier in the race.

Eventually, someone will run a marathon in less than two hours. The present record is 2:08:13. I believe that the first person to do so will run only about 90 miles a week. Rather than run more miles, his training will be more intense. For example, one of Salazar's drills is a 9-mile run [15 km.] on a mile loop, running a pace of alternating fast and slow miles. He will start by running 5:00 for the fast miles and 5:40 for the slow miles, running in sequence 5:00, then 5:40, then 5:00, then 5:40, and so on, with the ninth mile being 5:00. At peak, he will run the fast miles in 4:30 and the slow miles in 5:00. The idea is to develop the ability to surge, but also to get his body to think of a five-minute mile as a resting pace.

This training concept will hold true for the two-hour marathoner. His easy runs will be at five-minute pace for a mile; his training mileage will be lower than that of most marathoners, but the intensity will be much higher. He will also do supplementary work, such as bicycling, swimming, and strength and flexibility training, which will improve his body without stressing his legs and feet further. Naturally, the runner will not start out at or jump to such an intense level of training. It will be the culmination of some 10 to 20 years of increasing training loads being applied to a genetically gifted body.

You can get other ideas for marathon tactics from ideas suggested for the other running events. The length of the marathon gives plenty of time for using different tactics. Desire, careful planning and preparation will yield very good results in the marathon.

TACTICS FOR THE STEEPLECHASE

Perhaps fewer tactics are seen in steeplechase races than in races on the flat because the high degree of skill demanded by the barriers and water jumps requires all the runners' concentration. Accelerating before jumping a barrier or water jump is enough of a challenge without trying to throw in additional accelerations as a tactic.

Instead of competitive tactics, consider the following suggestions for running a steeplechase:

(1) In most cases, you are better off if you start the race at a conservative pace, running in a position where you have a good view of the next barrier or water jump, and staying clear of a tightly grouped pack of runners. If necessary, you should run wide as you approach the barrier, so you will have an unobstructed view.

(2) If you are much faster than your opponents, you should take the lead immediately to ensure yourself an unobstructed view.

(3) You might try using this tactic for surprise: Accelerate into the water jump with about 500 to 600 meters remaining in the race, then continue accelerating to the finish.

TACTICS FOR CROSS-COUNTRY

Cross-country is the one area of distance running where both individual and team tactics must be considered. We will look at both tactics.

Individual tactics. Each runner wants to do his or her best. If you are the number one runner on your team, you want to be competitive with the number one runner on the other team or teams. You need to become calloused to starting quickly to gain position, maintaining a good pace throughout the race, then finishing strongly. These skills can be developed in your workouts. Some other tactics you can use in cross-country are:

(1) Surge in the middle of the race to attempt to break away from the pack.

(2) Learn to run at a full, but controlled, speed on the downhill. Many runners try to rest on the downhills, which makes this a good time for a surprise move.

(3) Reverse the procedure by running harder on the uphill, then relaxing on the downhill.

(4) You should callous yourself to uneven-pace running. Cross-country can have big packs of runners, hills, and sharp turns, which will cause frequent changes of pace throughout the race.

Team tactics. Among the team tactics that can be used in cross-country are:

(1) Pick out the runner on the other team who ranks in the same place as you do on your team, key on him and try to finish ahead of him.

(2) Running together as a team has both good and bad points. It can help in keeping the slower team members motivated, but the team that runs together is not helping itself if the opponent's runners are ahead of you. And sometimes team members are far apart in their abilities. The faster runners should not hold back significantly to stay with the team, nor should slower runners be pushed beyond their abilities just to be in a pack. The result would be a team whose members did not run to their full capacities.

From reading these tactics and watching races, you will think of other tactics yourself. As you run more races and study other runners, you will learn far more tactics than you will ever need for successful racing. Just remember that the most important criterion of any winning tactic is surprise. You want your opponent to be unable to respond, or to know that if he does respond, it will weaken his own chances of winning. Be prepared to take advantage of surprise when you do achieve it.

11. Planning for the Future: Thinking Ahead

As we have already mentioned, if you set reasonable goals, plan your training program carefully, and train with moderation using the Oregon training principles, you will reach any reasonable goal you set. Once a goal is reached, you should then follow the same process of goal-setting as before. If you are near the end of a racing season, you should elevate your sights a bit. If the season is over, start planning for next year. Look at what you have accomplished and study your training records to see how you did it. Then you will be ready to set reasonable, realistic goals for the next year.

If you enjoy running, do not look at the goal-setting and program-planning process as a simple one-season or one-year event. Fit your running into your life goals, and plan on enjoying your sport for years to come. Don't set goals that are unreasonable, but don't sell yourself short either. You reach greater heights by aiming higher.

Making Adjustments When the Season is Over

When your racing season is over, give yourself a rest for recovery and recreation. Take up some of the activities you could not enjoy while training and racing. If you want to run regularly, just take easy, comfortable jogs; do not make them training sessions.

Taking a break for a few weeks or a month will leave you refreshed and ready to return to training with enthusiasm. You will be ready to start looking toward next year's races and goals. Just be sure to begin your training at a reduced level. You are starting a new year, not picking up at the same level where you ended the season. However, if you start a little higher up the ladder than you started last year, you'll climb higher than before. Good times lie before you. Plan to reach them and enjoy them.

Appendix A: Imperial Road Pace Table

Mile Pace	8 km	10 km	15 km	10 mi	20 km	½ mar	30 km	Marathon
4:30	22:23	27:58	41:57	45:00	55:56			
4:40	23:12	29:00	43:30	46:40	58:00	1:01:11	1:27:00	
4:50	24:02	30:02	45:03	48:20	1:00:04	1:03:22	1:30:06	2:06:44
5:00	24:52	31:04	46:37	50:00	1:02:09	1:05:33	1:33:13	2:11:06
5:10	25:41	32:07	48:10	51:40	1:04:13	1:07:44	1:36:19	2:15:28
5:20	26:31	33:09	49:43	53:20	1:06:17	1:09:55	1:39:26	2:19:50
5:30	27:21	34:11	51:16	55:00	1:08:21	1:12:06	1:42:32	2:24:13
5:40	28:10	35:13	52:49	56:40	1:10:26	1:14:18	1:45:38	2:28:35
5:50	29:00	36:15	54:23	58:20	1:12:30	1:16:29	1:48:45	2:32:57
6:00	29:50	37:17	55:56	60:00	1:14:34	1:18:40	1:51:51	2:37:19
6:10	30:40	38:19	57:29	1:01:40	1:16:39	1:20:51	1:54:58	2:41:41
6:20	31:29	39:22	59:02	1:03:20	1:18:43	1:23:02	1:58:04	2:46:04
6:30	32:19	40:24	1:00:35	1:05:00	1:20:47	1:25:13	2:01:10	2:50:26
6:40	33:09	41:26	1:02:09	1:06:40	1:22:51	1:27:24	2:04:17	2:54:48
6:50	33:58	42:28	1:03:42	1:08:20	1:24:56	1:29:35	2:07:23	2:59:10
7:00	34:48	43:30	1:05:15	1:10:00	1:27:00	1:31:46	2:10:30	3:03:32
7:10	35:38	44:32	1:06:48	1:11:40	1:29:04	1:33:57	2:13:36	3:07:54
7:20	36:28	45:34	1:08:21	1:13:20	1:31:08	1:36:09	2:16:42	3:12:17
7:30	37:17	46:37	1:09:55	1:15:00	1:33:13	1:38:20	2:19:49	3:16:39
7:40	38:07	47:39	1:11:28	1:16:40	1:35:17	1:40:31	2:22:55	3:21:01
7:50	38:57	48:41	1:13:01	1:18:20	1:37:21	1:42:42	2:26:02	3:25:23
8:00	39:46	49:43	1:14:34	1:20:00	1:39:26	1:44:53	2:29:08	3:29:45
8:10	40:36	50:45	1:16:07	1:21:40	1:41:30	1:47:04	2:32:15	3:34:08
8:20	41:26	51:47	1:17:41	1:23:20	1:43:34	1:49:15	2:35:21	3:38:30
8:30	42:16	52:49	1:19:14	1:25:00	1:45:38	1:51:26	2:38:27	3:42:52
8:40	43:05	53:52	1:20:47	1:26:40	1:47:43	1:53:37	2:41:34	3:47:14
8:50	43:55	54:54	1:22:20	1:28:20	1:49:47	1:55:48	2:44:40	3:51:36
9:00	44:45	55:56	1:23:53	1:30:00	1:51:51	1:57:59	2:47:47	3:55:59
10:00	49:43	1:02:09	1:33:13	1:40:00	2:04:17	2:11:06	3:06:25	4:22:12
11:00	54:41	1:08:21	1:42:32	1:50:00	2:16:42	2:24:13	3:25:04	4:48:25
12:00	59:39	1:14:34	1:51:51	2:00:00	2:29:08	2:37:19	3:43:42	5:14:38

Appendix B: 440-Yard Track Pace Table

440	800	1500	Mile	3 km	5 km	10 km
51	1:41.41					
52	1:43:40					
53	1:45.38					
54	1:47.37					
55	1:49.36					
56	1:51.35	3:28.78	3:44.0			
57	1:53.34	3:32.51	3:48.0			
58	1:55.33	3:36.24	3:52.0			
59	1:57.31	3:39.96	3:56.0			
60	1:59.30	3:43.69	4:00.0	7:27.39		
61	2:01.29	3:47.42	4:04.0	7:34.84		
62	2:03.28	3:51.15	4:08.0	7:42.30	12:50.50	
63	2:05.27	3:54.88	4:12.0	7:49.76	13:02.93	
64	2:07.26	3:58.61	4:16.0	7:57.21	13:15.35	
65	2:09.24	4:02.33	4:20.0	8:04.67	13:27.78	26:55.56
66	2:11.23	4:06.11	4:24.0	8:12.12	13:40.21	27:20.42
67	2:13.22	4:09.79	4:28.0	8:19.58	13:52.64	27:45.27
68	2:15.21	4:13.52	4:32.0	8:27.04	14:05.06	28:10.13
69	2:17.20	4:17.25	4:36.0	8:34.49	14:17.49	28:34.98
70	2:19.19	4:20.98	4:40.0	8:41.95	14:29.92	28:59.84
71	2:21.18	4:24.70	4:44.0	8:49.41	14:42.34	29:24.69
72	2:23.16	4:28.43	4:48.0	8:56.86	14:54.77	29:49.55
73	2:25.15	4:32.16	4:52.0	9:04.32	15:07.20	30:14.40
74	2:27.14	4:35.89	4:56.0	9:11.78	15:19.63	30:39.25
75	2:29.13	4:39.62	5:00.0	9:19.23	15:32.05	31:04.11
76	2:31.12	4:43.35	5:04.0	9:26.69	15:44.48	31:28.96

APPENDIX B: 440-YARD PACE TABLE
(continued)

440	800	1500	Mile	3 km	5 km	10 km
77	2:33.11	4:47.07	5:08.0	9:34.15	15:56.91	31:53.82
78	2:35.10	4:50.80	5:12.0	9:41.61	16:09.34	32:18.67
79	2:37.08	4:54.53	5:16.0	9:49.06	16:21.76	32:43.53
80	2:39.07	4:58.26	5:20.0	9:56.52	16:34.19	33:08.38
81	2:41.06	5:01.99	5:24.0	10:03.98	16:46.62	33:32.24
82	2:43.05	5:05.72	5:28.0	10:11.43	16:59.05	33:58.09
83	2:45.04	5:09.44	5:32.0	10:18.89	17:11.48	34:22.95
84	2:47.03	5:13.17	5:36.0	10:26.35	17:23.91	34:47.80
85	2:49.01	5:16.90	5:40.0	10:33.80	17:36.34	35:12.67
86	2:51.00	5:20.63	5:44.0	10:41.26	17:48.76	35:37.53
87	2:52.99	5:24.36	5:48.0	10:48.71	18:01.19	36:02.38
88	2:54.97	5:28.09	5:52.0	10:56.17	18:13.62	36:27.24
89	2:56.96	5:31.81	5:56.0	11:03.63	18:26.05	36:52.09
90	2:58.95	5:35.54	6:00.0	11:11.08	18:38.47	37:16.95

Appendix C: Metric Road Pace Table

Kilometer Pace	8 km	10 km	15 km	10 mi	20 km	½ mar	30 km	Marathon
2:40	21:20	26:40						
2:50	22:40	28:20						
3:00	24:00	30:00	45:00	48:17	1:00:00	1:03:18	1:30:00	2:06:35
3:10	25:20	31:40	47:30	50:58	1:03:20	1:06:49	1:35:00	2:13:37
3:20	26:40	33:20	50:00	53:39	1:06:40	1:10:20	1:40:00	2:20:39
3:30	28:00	35:00	52:30	56:20	1:10:00	1:13:51	1:45:00	2:27:41
3:40	29:20	36:40	55:00	59:01	1:13:20	1:17:22	1:50:00	2:34:43
3:50	30:40	38:20	57:30	1:01:42	1:16:40	1:20:53	1:55:00	2:41:45
4:00	32:00	40:00	1:00:00	1:04:23	1:20:00	1:24:24	2:00:00	2:48:47
4:10	33:20	41:40	1:02:30	1:07:04	1:23:20	1:27:55	2:05:00	2:55:49
4:20	34:40	43:40	1:05:00	1:09:45	1:26:40	1:31:26	2:10:00	3:02:51
4:30	36:00	45:00	1:07:30	1:12:26	1:30:00	1:34:57	2:15:00	3:09:53
4:40	37:20	46:40	1:10:00	1:15:07	1:33:20	1:38:28	2:20:00	3:16:55
4:50	38:40	48:20	1:12:30	1:17:47	1:36:40	1:41:59	2:25:00	3:23:57
5:00	40:00	50:00	1:15:00	1:20:28	1:40:00	1:45:30	2:30:00	3:30:59
5:10	41:20	51:40	1:17:30	1:23:09	1:43:20	1:49:01	2:35:00	3:38:01
5:20	42:40	53:20	1:20:00	1:25:50	1:46:40	1:52:32	2:40:00	3:45:03
5:30	44:00	55:00	1:22:30	1:28:31	1:50:00	1:56:03	2:45:00	3:52:05
5:40	45:20	56:40	1:25:00	1:31:12	1:53:20	1:59:34	2:50:00	3:59:07
5:50	46:40	58:20	1:27:30	1:33:53	1:56:40	2:03:05	2:55:00	4:06:09
6:00	48:00	1:00:00	1:30:00	1:36:34	2:00:00	2:06:35	3:00:00	4:13:11
7:00	56:00	1:10:00	1:45:00	1:52:40	2:20:00	2:27:41	3:30:00	4:55:22
8:00	1:04:00	1:20:00	2:00:00	2:08:45	2:40:00	2:48:47	4:00:00	5:37:34

Appendix D: 400-Meter Track Pace Table

400	800	1 km	1500	Mile	2 km	3 km	5 km	10 km
51	1:42							
52	1:44	2:10.0						
53	1:46	2:12.5						
54	1:48	2:15.0						
55	1:50	2:17.5	3:26.25	3:41.28				
56	1:52	2:20.0	3:30.0	3:45.31				
57	1:54	2:22.5	3:33.75	3:49.33	4:45			
58	1:56	2:25.0	3:37.5	3:53.35	4:50			
59	1:58	2:27.5	3:41.25	3:57.38	4:55			
60	2:00	2:30.0	3:45.0	4:01.40	5:00	7:30.0		
61	2:02	2:32.5	3:48.75	4:05.42	5:05	7:37.5		
62	2:04	2:35.0	3:52.5	4:09.45	5:10	7:45.0	12:55.0	
63	2:06	2:37.5	3:56.25	4:13.47	5:15	7:52.5	13:07.5	
64	2:08	2:40.0	4:00.0	4:17.5	5:20	8:00.0	13:20.0	
65	2:10	2:42.5	4:03.75	4:21.52	5:25	8:07.5	13:32.5	27:05
66	2:12	2:45.0	4:07.5	4:25.54	5:30	8:15.0	13:45.0	27:30
67	2:14	2:47.5	4:11.25	4:29.57	5:35	8:22.5	13:57.5	27:55
68	2:16	2:50.0	4:15.0	4:33.59	5:40	8:30.0	14:10.0	28:20
69	2:18	2:52.5	4:18.75	4:37.61	5:45	8:37.5	14:22.5	28:45
70	2:20	2:55.0	4:22.5	4:41.64	5:50	8:45.0	14:35.0	29:10
71	2:22	2:57.5	4:26.25	4:45.66	5:55	8:52.5	14:47.5	29:35
72	2:24	3:00.0	4:30.0	4:49.68	6:00	9:00.0	15:00.0	30:00

APPENDIX D: 400-METER PACE TABLE
(continued)

400	800	1 km	1500	Mile	2 km	3 km	5 km	10 km
73	2:26	3:02.5	4:33.75	4:53.71	6:05	9:07.5	15:12.5	30:25
74	2:28	3:05.0	4:37.5	4:57.73	6:10	9:15.0	15:25.0	30:50
75	2:30	3:07.5	4:41.25	5:01.75	6:15	9:22.5	15:37.5	31:15
76	2:32	3:10.0	4:45.0	5:05.78	6:20	9:30.0	15:50.0	31:40
77	2:34	3:12.5	4:48.75	5:09.80	6:25	9:37.5	16:02.5	32:05
78	2:36	3:15.0	4:52.5	5:13.82	6:30	9:45.0	16:15.0	32:30
79	2:38	3:17.5	4:56.25	5:17.85	6:35	9:52.5	16:27.5	32:55
80	2:40	3:20.0	5:00.0	5:21.87	6:40	10:00.0	16:40.0	33:20
81	2:42	3:22.5	5:03.75	5:25.89	6:45	10:07.5	16:52.5	33:45
82	2:44	3:25.0	5:07.5	5:29.92	6:50	10:15.0	17:05.0	34:10
83	2:46	3:27.5	5:11.25	5:33.94	6:55	10:22.5	17:17.5	34:35
84	2:48	3:30.0	5:15.0	5:37.96	7:00	10:30.0	17:30.0	35:00
85	2:50	3:32.5	5:18.75	5:41.99	7:05	10:37.5	17:42.5	35:25
86	2:52	3:35.0	5:22.5	5:46.01	7:10	10:45.0	17:55.0	35:50
87	2:54	3:37.5	5:26.25	5:50.03	7:15	10:52.5	18:07.5	36:15
88	2:56	3:40.0	5:30.0	5:54.06	7:20	11:00.0	18:20.0	36:40
89	2:58	3:42.5	5:33.75	5:58.08	7:25	11:07.5	18:32.5	37:05
90	3:00	3:45.0	5:37.5	6:02.10	7:30	11:15.0	18:45.0	37:30

Appendix E: Comparative Performance Tables Road Racing

by J. Gerry Purdy

Pts	8 km	10 km	15 km	10 mi	20 km	½ mar	30 km	Marathon
1050	21:46	27:37	42:33	45:53	57:49	1:01:12	1:29:03	2:08:30
1040	21:53	27:46	42:47	46:09	58:08	1:01:33	1:29:34	2:09:14
1030	22:00	27:56	43:02	46:25	58:29	1:01:55	1:30:05	2:10:00
1020	22:08	28:05	43:17	46:41	58:49	1:02:16	1:30:36	2:10:46
1010	22:16	28:15	43:32	46:57	59:09	1:02:38	1:31:08	2:11:32
1000	22:23	28:25	43:47	47:13	59:30	1:03:00	1:31:41	2:12:19
990	22:31	28:35	44:02	47:30	59:51	1:03:22	1:32:13	2:13:06
980	22:39	28:45	44:18	47:47	1:00:13	1:03:44	1:32:46	2:13:54
970	22:47	28:55	44:34	48:04	1:00:34	1:04:08	1:33:20	2:14:43
960	22:55	29:05	44:50	48:21	1:00:56	1:04:31	1:33:54	2:15:32
950	23:03	29:15	45:06	48:39	1:01:18	1:04:54	1:34:28	2:16:22
940	23:11	29:26	45:22	48:56	1:01:41	1:05:18	1:35:03	2:17:12
930	23:20	29:37	45:39	49:14	1:02:03	1:05:41	1:35:38	2:18:04
920	23:28	29:47	45:56	49:32	1:02:26	1:06:07	1:36:14	2:18:55
910	23:37	29:58	46:13	49:51	1:02:49	1:06:31	1:36:50	2:19:48
900	23:45	30:09	46:30	50:09	1:03:13	1:06:56	1:37:26	2:20:41
890	23:54	30:21	46:47	50:28	1:03:37	1:07:22	1:38:03	2:21:34
880	24:03	30:32	47:05	50:47	1:04:01	1:07:46	1:38:40	2:22:29
870	24:12	30:43	47:23	51:06	1:04:25	1:08:13	1:39:18	2:23:24
860	24:21	30:55	47:41	51:26	1:04:50	1:08:38	1:39:57	2:24:20
850	24:30	31:07	47:59	51:46	1:05:15	1:09:05	1:40:36	2:25:16

APPENDIX E
COMPARATIVE PERFORMANCE TABLES

ROAD RACING DISTANCES
Listed by whole seconds
(continued)

Pts	8 km	10 km	15 km	10 mi	20 km	½ mar	30 km	Marathon
840	24:40	31:19	48:18	52:06	1:05:40	1:09:31	1:41:15	2:26:13
830	24:49	31:31	48:36	52:26	1:06:06	1:09:59	1:41:55	2:27:11
820	24:59	31:43	48:55	53:07	1:06:32	1:10:27	1:42:35	2:28:10
810	25:09	31:55	49:15	53:28	1:06:58	1:10:54	1:43:16	2:29:10
800	25:18	32:08	49:34	53:39	1:07:25	1:11:22	1:43:58	2:30:10
790	25:28	32:21	49:54	53:50	1:07:52	1:11:51	1:44:40	2:31:11
780	25:38	32:33	50:14	54:11	1:08:19	1:12:21	1:45:22	2:32:13
770	25:49	32:46	50:34	54:33	1:08:47	1:12:50	1:46:06	2:33:16
760	25:59	33:00	50:55	54:55	1:09:15	1:13:19	1:46:50	2:34:20
750	26:09	33:13	51:16	55:18	1:09:55	1:13:50	1:47:34	2:35:25
740	26:20	33:27	51:37	55:41	1:10:13	1:14:21	1:48:19	2:36:30
730	26:31	33:40	51:58	56:04	1:10:42	1:14:52	1:49:05	2:37:37
720	26:42	33:54	52:20	56:28	1:11:12	1:15:24	1:49:51	2:38:44
710	26:53	34:09	52:42	56:51	1:11:42	1:15:56	1:50:38	2:39:53
700	27:04	34:23	53:05	57:16	1:12:13	1:16:28	1:51:26	2:41:02
690	27:16	34:38	53:27	57:40	1:12:44	1:17:01	1:52:14	2:42:13
680	27:27	34:52	53:50	58:05	1:13:15	1:17:35	1:53:03	2:43:24
670	27:39	35:07	54:14	58:30	1:13:47	1:18:08	1:53:53	2:44:37
660	27:51	35:22	54:37	58:56	1:14:20	1:18:42	1:54:43	2:45:50
650	28:03	35:38	55:01	59:22	1:14:53	1:19:17	1:55:35	2:47:05
640	28:15	35:53	55:26	59:48	1:15:26	1:19:53	1:56:27	2:48:21
630	28:27	36:09	55:51	1:00:15	1:16:00	1:20:29	1:57:19	2:49:38
620	28:40	36:25	56:16	1:00:42	1:16:35	1:21:05	1:58:13	2:50:56
610	28:53	36:42	56:41	1:01:10	1:17:10	1:21:43	1:59:08	2:52:15
600	29:06	36:58	57:07	1:01:38	1:17:45	1:22:20	2:00:03	2:53:36
590	29:19	37:15	57:33	1:02:06	1:18:21	1:22:58	2:00:59	2:54:58
580	29:32	37:32	58:00	1:02:35	1:18:58	1:23:37	2:01:56	2:56:21
570	29:46	37:50	58:27	1:03:04	1:19:35	1:24:16	2:02:54	2:57:45
560	30:00	38:07	58:55	1:03:34	1:20:13	1:24:56	2:03:53	2:59:11
550	30:14	38:25	59:23	1:04:04	1:20:51	1:25:36	2:04:53	3:00:39

APPENDIX E
COMPARATIVE PERFORMANCE TABLES

ROAD RACING DISTANCES
Listed by whole seconds
(continued)

Pts	8 km	10 km	15 km	10 mi	20 km	½ mar	30 km	Marathon
540	30:28	38:43	59:51	1:04:35	1:21:30	1:26:18	2:05:53	3:02:07
530	30:42	39:02	1:00:20	1:05:06	1:22:10	1:27:00	2:06:55	3:03:37
520	30:57	39:21	1:00:49	1:05:38	1:22:50	1:27:42	2:07:58	3:05:09
510	31:12	39:40	1:01:19	1:06:10	1:23:31	1:28:26	2:09:02	3:06:42
500	31:27	39:59	1:01:50	1:06:43	1:24:12	1:29:10	2:10:07	3:08:17
490	31:43	40:19	1:02:20	1:07:16	1:24:55	1:29:55	2:11:13	3:09:53
480	31:58	40:39	1:02:52	1:07:50	1:25:38	1:30:40	2:12:20	3:11:32
470	32:14	40:59	1:03:24	1:08:24	1:26:21	1:31:27	2:13:28	3:13:11
460	32:30	41:20	1:03:56	1:08:59	1:27:06	1:32:14	2:14:38	3:14:53
450	32:47	41:41	1:04:29	1:09:35	1:27:51	1:33:03	2:15:48	3:16:36
440	33:04	42:03	1:05:03	1:10:11	1:28:37	1:33:51	2:17:00	3:18:21
430	33:21	42:24	1:05:37	1:10:48	1:29:24	1:34:41	2:18:14	3:20:08
420	33:38	42:47	1:06:11	1:11:26	1:30:12	1:35:31	2:19:28	3:21:57
410	33:56	43:09	1:06:47	1:12:04	1:31:00	1:36:24	2:20:44	3:23:48
400	34:14	43:32	1:07:23	1:12:43	1:31:50	1:37:15	2:22:01	3:25:41
390	34:32	43:55	1:07:59	1:13:22	1:32:40	1:38:09	2:23:20	3:27:36
380	34:50	44:19	1:08:37	1:14:03	1:33:31	1:39:03	2:24:40	3:29:34
370	35:09	44:43	1:09:15	1:14:44	1:34:24	1:39:59	2:26:02	3:31:33
360	35:29	45:08	1:09:53	1:15:26	1:35:17	1:40:55	2:27:25	3:33:35
350	35:48	45:33	1:10:33	1:16:08	1:36:11	1:41:53	2:28:50	3:35:39
340	36:08	45:59	1:11:13	1:16:52	1:37:06	1:42:51	2:30:16	3:37:46
330	36:29	46:25	1:11:54	1:17:36	1:38:02	1:43:51	2:31:44	3:39:55
320	36:49	46:52	1:12:36	1:18:21	1:39:00	1:44:52	2:33:14	3:42:06
310	37:11	47:19	1:13:18	1:19:07	1:39:58	1:45:54	2:34:46	3:44:21
300	37:32	47:46	1:14:02	1:19:54	1:40:58	1:46:57	2:36:20	3:46:38
290	37:54	48:15	1:14:46	1:20:42	1:41:59	1:48:01	2:37:55	3:48:58
280	38:16	48:43	1:15:31	1:21:31	1:43:01	1:49:07	2:39:32	3:51:21
270	38:39	49:13	1:16:17	1:22:21	1:44:05	1:50:14	2:41:12	3:53:46
260	39:03	49:43	1:17:04	1:23:12	1:45:09	1:51:23	2:42:53	3:56:15
250	39:26	50:13	1:17:52	1:24:03	1:46:15	1:52:34	2:44:37	3:58:47

APPENDIX E
COMPARATIVE PERFORMANCE TABLES

ROAD RACING DISTANCES
Listed by whole seconds
(continued)

Pts	8 km	10 km	15 km	10 mi	20 km	½ mar	30 km	Marathon
240	39:51	50:44	1:18:41	1:24:56	1:47:23	1:53:46	2:46:23	4:01:23
230	40:16	51:16	1:19:31	1:25:51	1:48:32	1:54:58	2:48:11	4:04:02
220	40:41	51:49	1:20:22	1:26:46	1:49:42	1:56:13	2:50:02	4:06:44
210	41:07	52:22	1:21:15	1:27:42	1:50:54	1:57:29	2:51:55	4:09:30
200	41:33	52:56	1:22:08	1:28:40	1:52:08	1:58:47	2:53:50	4:12:20
190	42:00	53:30	1:23:02	1:29:39	1:53:23	2:00:06	2:55:48	4:15:13
180	42:28	54:06	1:23:58	1:30:39	1:54:40	2:01:28	2:57:49	4:18:11
170	42:56	54:42	1:24:55	1:31:41	1:55:59	2:02:51	2:59:53	4:21:13
160	43:25	55:19	1:25:54	1:32:44	1:57:19	2:04:16	3:02:00	4:24:19
150	43:54	55:57	1:26:53	1:33:49	1:58:41	2:05:44	3:04:09	4:27:29
140	44:24	56:35	1:27:54	1:34:55	2:00:06	2:07:14	3:06:22	4:30:45
130	44:55	57:15	1:28:57	1:36:03	2:01:32	2:08:45	3:08:38	4:34:05
120	45:26	57:56	1:30:01	1:37:12	2:03:00	2:10:19	3:10:57	4:37:30
110	45:59	58:37	1:31:06	1:38:23	2:04:31	2:11:56	3:13:20	4:41:00
100	46:32	59:20	1:32:14	1:39:36	2:06:04	2:13:34	3:15:46	4:44:36
90	47:06	60:03	1:33:23	1:40:50	2:07:39	2:15:16	3:18:16	4:48:17
80	47:40	60:48	1:34:33	1:42:07	2:09:17	2:16:58	3:20:50	4:52:04
70	48:16	61:34	1:35:46	1:43:25	2:10:57	2:18:45	3:23:28	4:55:57
60	48:52	62:21	1:37:00	1:44:45	2:12:40	2:20:14	3:26:10	4:59:56
50	49:30	63:09	1:38:16	1:46:08	2:14:25	2:22:26	3:28:57	5:04:02
40	50:08	63:58	1:39:34	1:47:33	2:16:13	2:24:21	3:31:48	5:08:15
30	50:04	64:49	1:40:55	1:49:00	2:18:05	2:26:19	3:34:44	5:12:34
20	51:28	65:41	1:42:17	1:50:29	2:19:59	2:28:20	3:37:45	5:17:01
10	52:09	66:34	1:43:32	1:52:01	2:21:56	2:31:25	3:40:50	5:21:36
0	52:52	67:29	1:45:09	1:53:35	2:23:57	2:32:33	3:44:02	5:26:19

Appendices E and F are modified from the scoring tables developed by J. Gerry Purdy and included in James B. Gardner and J. Gerry Purdy's *Computerized Running Training Programs* (Tafnews Press, 1970). They are used with the permission of Tafnews Press.

Appendix F: Comparative Performance Tables Track Racing

by J. Gerry Purdy

Pts	800	1 km	1500 m	Mile	3 km	2 Miles	5 km	10 km
1080	1:40.6	2:10.7	3:27.8	3:45.1	7:29.3	8:05.1	12:58.2	27:08.7
1070	1:41.1	2:11.4	3:28.9	3:46.3	7:31.7	8:07.7	13:02.5	27:17.8
1060	1:41.6	2:12.0	3:30.0	3:47.5	7:34.2	8:10.4	13:06.8	27:27.0
1050	1:42.2	2:12.7	3:31.1	3:48.8	7:36.7	8:13.1	13:11.2	27:36.2
1040	1:42.7	2:13.4	3:32.2	3:50.0	7:39.2	8:15.8	13:15.6	27:45.6
1030	1:43.2	2:14.1	3:33.4	3:51.2	7:41.8	8:18.5	13:20.1	27:55.1
1020	1:43.8	2:14.8	3:34.5	3:52.5	7:44.3	8:21.3	13:24.6	28:04.7
1010	1:44.3	2:15.6	3:35.7	3:53.8	7:46.9	8:24.1	13:29.2	28:14.4
1000	1:44.9	2:16.3	3:36.9	3:55.1	7:49.6	8:27.0	13:33.8	28:24.2
990	1:45.4	2:17.0	3:38.1	3:56.4	7:52.2	8:29.9	13:38.5	28:34.1
980	1:46.0	2:17.8	3:39.3	3:57.7	7:54.9	8:32.8	13:43.2	28:44.1
970	1:46.6	2:18.5	3:40.5	3:59.0	7:57.7	8:35.7	13:48.0	28:54.3
960	1:47.1	2:19.3	3:41.8	4:00.4	8:00.4	8:38.7	13:52.8	29:04.6
950	1:47.7	2:20.0	3:43.0	4:01.7	8:03.2	8:41.7	13:57.7	29:15.0
940	1:48.3	2:20.8	3:44.3	4:03.1	8:06.0	8:44.8	14:02.7	29:25.5
930	1:48.9	2:21.6	3:45.6	4:04.5	8:08.9	8:47.9	14:07.7	29:36.2
920	1:49.5	2:22.4	3:46.8	4:05.9	8:11.8	8:51.0	14:12.8	29:47.0
910	1:50.1	2:23.2	3:48.2	4:07.3	8:14.7	8:54.2	14:17.9	29:57.9
900	1:50.7	2:24.0	3:49.5	4:08.8	8:17.7	8:57.4	14:23.1	30:08.9

APPENDIX F:
COMPARATIVE PERFORMANCE TABLES

TRACK RACING DISTANCES
(continued)

Pts	800	1 km	1500 m	Mile	3 km	2 Miles	5 km	10 km
890	1:51.3	2:24.8	3:50.8	4:10.2	8:20.6	9:00.6	14:28.3	30:20.1
880	1:52.0	2:25.7	3:52.2	4:11.7	8:23.7	9:03.9	14:33.7	30:31.4
870	1:52.6	2:26.5	3:53.6	4:13.2	8:26.7	9:07.2	14:39.1	30:42.9
860	1:53.2	2:27.3	3:54.9	4:14.7	8:29.8	9:10.6	14:44.5	30:54.5
850	1:53.9	2:28.2	3:56.3	4:16.2	8:33.0	9:14.0	14:50.0	31:06.3
840	1:54.5	2:29.1	3:57.8	4:17.8	8:36.2	9:17.4	14:55.6	31:18.2
830	1:55.2	2:30.0	3:59.2	4:19.3	8:39.4	9:20.9	15:01.3	31:30.3
820	1:55.9	2:30.8	4:00.7	4:20.9	8:42.7	9:24.4	15:07.1	31:42.5
810	1:56.5	2:31.7	4:02.1	4:22.5	8:46.0	9:28.0	15:12.9	31:54.9
800	1:57.2	2:32.7	4:03.6	4:24.1	8:49.3	9:31.6	15:18.8	32:07.4
790	1:57.9	2:33.6	4:05.1	4:25.8	8:52.7	9:35.3	15:24.7	32:20.1
780	1:58.6	2:34.5	4:06.7	4:27.4	8:56.1	9:39.0	15:30.8	32:33.0
770	1:59.3	2:35.5	4:08.2	4:29.1	8:59.6	9:42.8	15:36.9	32:46.0
760	2:00.1	2:36.4	4:09.8	4:30.8	9:03.1	9:46.6	15:43.1	32:59.3
750	2:00.8	2:37.4	4:11.4	4:32.6	9:06.7	9:50.4	15:49.4	33:12.7
740	2:01.5	2:38.4	4:13.0	4:34.3	9:10.7	9:54.3	15:55.7	33:26.3
730	2:02.3	2:39.4	4:14.6	4:36.1	9:14.0	9:58.3	16:02.2	33:40.0
720	2:03.0	2:40.4	4:16.3	4:37.9	9:17.7	10:02.3	16:08.7	33:54.0
710	2:03.8	2:41.4	4:17.9	4:39.7	9:21.4	10:06.4	16:15.4	34:08.1
700	2:04.6	2:42.4	4:19.6	4:41.6	9:25.3	10:10.5	16:22.1	34:22.5
690	2:05.4	2:43.5	4:21.4	4:43.4	9:29.1	10:14.7	16:28.9	34:37.1
680	2:06.2	2:44.5	4:23.1	4:45.3	9:33.0	10:19.0	16:35.8	34:51.8
670	2:07.0	2:45.6	4:24.9	4:47.2	9:37.0	10:23.3	16:42.8	35:06.8
660	2:07.8	2:46.7	4:26.7	4:49.2	9:41.0	10:27.6	16:49.9	35:22.0
650	2:08.6	2:47.8	4:28.5	4:51.2	9:45.1	10:32.0	16:57.2	35:37.4

APPENDIX F:
COMPARATIVE PERFORMANCE TABLES

TRACK RACING DISTANCES
(continued)

Pts	800	1 km	1500 m	Mile	3 km	2 Miles	5 km	10 km
640	2:09.5	2:48.9	4:30.3	4:53.2	9:49.3	10:36.5	17:04.5	35:53.0
630	2:10.3	2:50.0	4:32.2	4:55.2	9:53.5	10:41.1	17:11.9	36:08.9
620	2:11.2	2:51.2	4:34.0	4:57.2	9:57.7	10:45.7	17:19.4	36:25.0
610	2:12.0	2:52.3	4:36.0	4:59.3	10:02.1	10:50.4	17:27.1	36:41.4
600	2:12.9	2:53.5	4:37.9	5:01.4	10:06.4	10:55.1	17:34.8	36:57.9
590	2:13.8	2:54.7	4:39.9	5:03.6	10:10.9	10:59.9	17:42.7	37:14.8
580	2:14.7	2:55.9	4:41.9	5:05.8	10:15.4	11:04.8	17:50.7	37:31.9
570	2:15.6	2:57.1	4:43.9	5:08.0	10:20.0	11:09.8	17:58.8	37:49.3
560	2:16.6	2:58.4	4:46.0	5:10.2	10:24.7	11:14.8	18:07.0	38:06.9
550	2:17.5	2:59.6	4:48.0	5:12.5	10:29.4	11:20.0	18:15.4	38:24.8
540	2:18.5	3:00.9	4:50.1	5:14.8	10:34.2	11:25.2	18:23.9	38:43.0
530	2:19.4	3:02.2	4:52.3	5:17.1	10:39.0	11:30.4	18:32.5	39:01.5
520	2:20.4	3:03.5	4:54.5	5:19.5	10:44.0	11:35.8	18:41.2	39:20.3
510	2:21.4	3:04.9	4:56.7	5:21.9	10:49.0	11:41.2	18:50.1	39:39.3
500	2:22.4	3:06.2	4:58.9	5:24.3	10:54.1	11:46.8	18:59.2	39:58.7
490	2:23.5	3:07.6	5:01.2	5:26.8	10:59.3	11:52.4	19:08.3	40:18.4
480	2:24.5	3:09.0	5:03.5	5:29.3	11:04.6	11:58.1	19:17.7	40:38.5
470	2:25.6	3:10.4	5:05.9	5:31.9	11:09.9	12:03.9	19:27.2	40:58.9
460	2:26.6	3:11.9	5:08.3	5:34.5	11:15.3	12:09.8	19:36.8	41:19.6
450	2:27.7	3:13.3	5:10.7	5:37.1	11:20.9	12:15.7	19:46.6	41:40.7
440	2:28.8	3:14.8	5:13.1	5:39.8	11:26.5	12:21.8	19:56.6	42:02.1
430	2:30.0	3:16.3	5:15.6	5:42.5	11:32.2	12:28.0	20:06.7	42:23.9
420	2:31.1	3:17.8	5:18.2	5:45.3	11:38.0	12:34.3	20:17.0	42:46.1
410	2:32.3	3:19.4	5:20.8	5:48.1	11:43.9	12:40.7	20:27.5	43:08.6
400	2:33.4	3:21.0	5:23.4	5:51.0	11:49.9	12:47.2	20:38.2	43:31.6

APPENDIX F:
COMPARATIVE PERFORMANCE TABLES

TRACK RACING DISTANCES
(continued)

Pts	800	1 km	1500 m	Mile	3 km	2 Miles	5 km	10 km
390	2:34.6	3:22.6	5:26.1	5:53.9	11:56.0	12:53.8	20:49.0	43:55.0
380	2:35.8	3:24.2	5:28.8	5:56.9	12:02.2	13:00.6	21:00.1	44:18.8
370	2:37.1	3:25.8	5:31.5	5:59.9	12:08.6	13:07.4	21:11.3	44:43.0
360	2:38.3	3:27.5	5:34.3	6:02.9	12:15.0	13:14.4	21:22.8	45:07.7
350	2:39.6	3:29.2	5:37.2	6:06.0	12:21.5	13:21.5	21:34.4	45:32.9
340	2:40.9	3:31.0	5:40.1	6:09.2	12:28.2	13:28.7	21:46.3	45:58.5
330	2:42.2	3:32.7	5:43.1	6:12.4	12:35.0	13:36.1	21:58.4	46:24.6
320	2:43.5	3:34.5	5:46.1	6:15.7	12:41.9	13:43.6	22:10.7	46:51.2
310	2:44.9	3:36.4	5:49.1	6:19.0	12:49.0	13:51.2	22:23.3	47:18.3
300	2:46.3	3:38.2	5:52.2	6:22.4	12:56.1	13:59.0	22:36.0	47:46.0
290	2:47.7	3:40.1	5:55.4	6:25.9	13:03.4	14:06.9	22:49.1	48:14.1
280	2:49.1	3:42.0	5:58.6	6:29.4	13:10.9	14:15.0	23:02.4	48:42.9
270	2:50.5	3:44.0	6:01.9	6:33.0	13:18.5	14:23.2	23:15.9	49:12.2
260	2:52.0	3:46.0	6:05.3	6:36.6	13:26.2	14:31.6	23:29.7	49:42.1
250	2:53.5	3:48.0	6:08.7	6:40.4	13:34.1	14:40.1	23:43.8	50:12.7
240	2:55.1	3:50.1	6:12.1	6:44.2	13:42.1	14:48.9	23:58.2	50:43.8
230	2:56.6	3:52.2	6:15.7	6:48.0	13:50.3	14:57.8	24:12.8	51:15.6
220	2:58.2	3:54.3	6:19.3	6:52.0	13:58.7	15:06.8	24:27.8	51:48.1
210	2:59.8	3:56.5	6:23.0	6:56.0	14:07.2	15:16.1	24:43.1	52:21.3
200	3:01.4	3:58.7	6:26.7	7:00.1	14:15.9	15:25.6	24:58.7	52:55.2
190	3:03.1	4:01.0	6:30.5	7:04.2	14:24.8	15:35.2	25:14.6	53:29.8
180	3:04.8	4:03.3	6:34.4	7:08.5	14:33.9	15:45.1	25:30.9	54:05.2
170	3:06.6	4:05.6	6:38.4	7:12.8	14:43.2	15:55.1	25:47.5	54:41.4
160	3:08.3	4:08.0	6:42.5	7:17.3	14:52.7	16:05.4	26:04.5	55:18.4
150	3:10.1	4:10.5	6:46.6	7:21.8	15:02.4	16:15.9	26:21.9	55:56.3

APPENDIX F:
COMPARATIVE PERFORMANCE TABLES

TRACK RACING DISTANCES
(continued)

Pts	800	1 km	1500 m	Mile	3 km	2 Miles	5 km	10 km
140	3:12.0	4:13.0	6:50.8	7:26.4	15:12.2	16:26.7	26:39.7	56:35.0
130	3:13.8	4:15.5	6:55.1	7:31.1	15:22.4	16:37.6	26:57.8	57:14.6
120	3:15.7	4:18.1	6:59.6	7:35.9	15:32.7	16:48.9	27:16.4	57:55.2
110	3:17.7	4:20.8	7:04.1	7:40.9	15:43.3	17:00.3	27:35.4	58:36.7
100	3:19.7	4:23.5	7:08.7	7:45.9	15:54.1	17:12.1	27:54.9	59:19.2
90	3:21.7	4:26.2	7:13.4	7:51.0	16:05.1	17:24.1	28:14.8	60:02.8
80	3:23.8	4:29.1	7:18.2	7:56.3	16:16.5	17:36.4	28:35.2	60:47.4
70	3:25.9	4:31.9	7:23.1	8:01.7	16:28.1	17:49.0	28:56.2	61:33.2
60	3:28.0	4:34.9	7:28.1	8:07.2	16:39.9	18:01.9	29:17.6	62:20.2
50	3:30.2	4:37.9	7:33.2	8:12.8	16:52.1	18:15.1	29:39.5	63:08.3
40	3:32.5	4:41.0	7:38.5	8:18.5	17:04.6	18:28.6	30:02.0	63:57.7
30	3:34.8	4:44.1	7:43.9	8:24.4	17:17.3	18:42.5	30:25.1	64:48.4
20	3:37.1	4:47.3	7:49.4	8:30.4	17:30.4	18:56.7	30:48.8	65:40.5
10	3:39.5	4:50.6	7:55.0	8:36.6	17:43.8	19:11.3	31:13.1	66:34.0
0	3:42.0	4:54.0	8:00.8	8:43.0	17:57.6	19:26.3	31:38.1	67:28.9

ABOUT THE AUTHORS

BILL DELLINGER

Bill Dellinger's involvement with running spans more than 35 years. His achievements as a runner rival those as a coach. The three-time Olympian (1956, '60, '64) capped his running career by winning the bronze medal in the 5000 meters in 1964. He won the NCAA mile in 1954, was the 2-mile champion in 1955 and the 5000 meters champion in 1956. He has held American records for 1500, 3000, 5000 meters and two miles, and held the indoor world record for the two- and three-mile. Dellinger has coached numerous world-class runners, including Alberto Salazar, Matt Centrowitz, Steve Prefontaine, Julie Brown, Bill McChesney and Rudy Chapa. Since becoming head coach at the University of Oregon in 1973, Dellinger's teams have captured the NCAA cross-country title three times and the track-and-field championship in 1984. He is the author of *The Running Experience* and *Winning Running*. Dellinger lives in Eugene, Ore.

BILL FREEMAN

Bill Freeman is a writer and coach living in Durham, N.C. Freeman is no stranger to the Oregon training system espoused by Dellinger and Bill Bowerman, having used it for 15 years in his own coaching. His Ph.D. dissertation in physical education at the University of Oregon was on Bowerman. Freeman is co-author of *Coaching Track and Field,* with Bowerman, and wrote *Physical Education in a Changing Society,* and *Physical Education and Sport in a Changing Society.* Freeman's wife, Jennifer, was a nationally ranked runner in the late 1970s.